Nation on Borrowed Time

Canada's Continental Destiny

Nicholas Ierullo

Contents

To the memory of Polybius; his native land was in the shadow of Rome.

Also by the author:

The Fall of the European Union and the Rise of the North American Union (2018)

The Clausewitz Manifesto (2017)

Introduction

"Perhaps we should rejoice in the disappearance of Canada. We leave the narrow provincialism and our backwoods culture; we enter the excitement of the United States where all the great things are being done. Who would compare the science, the art, the politics, the entertainment of our petty world to the overflowing achievements of New York, Washington, Chicago, and San Francisco? Think of William Faulkner and then think of Morley Callaghan. Think of the Kennedys and the Rockefellers and then think of Pearson and E. P. Taylor. This is the profoundest argument for the Liberals. They governed so as to break down our parochialism and lead us into the future.[1]"

This book is not another lament for a nation; it's a tired sigh in the face of the inevitable. George Grant's 1965 book was a lament for a nation whose destiny was already decided by forces both personal and impersonal and ultimately determined by the historical realities of power. Power, its use and the inevitable struggle to obtain and retain it, is the deciding factor in the development of history. When George Grant wrote his lament for Canada it was at a time when Canada and the rest of the world was in the middle of a geopolitical competition with stakes as

---

[1] Grant, G. (1970). *Lament for a Nation*. Toronto: McClelland and Stewart Limited in association with the Institute of Canadian Studies, Carleton University, pg. 88

high as the possibility of nuclear war and the future trajectory of the human race. Now, as Canada once again prepares itself for another election year[2], the world has returned to a state of great power competition; a struggle over the fate of the world order that Canada along with many other liberal-democratic regimes have spent so much blood and treasure to create.

The idea that the liberal world order, which Canada is undeniably a core member and defender of, is being challenged may be too much for those faint hearted Canadians who have come to believe that liberal-democracy married to the economic free market[3] is the *only* acceptable form of government because of its inherent morality and inevitable triumph. Since Grant's time Canada has become a much more vocal supporter of the world order forged by American leadership following Allied victory in the Second World War. But the more Canada identified with the liberal order the weaker the possibility of a Canadian identity became. In the 1960's, to Grant's dismay, Canada had not only accepted the American order but also Canada's "junior" position in the American-Canadian relationship culminating in Canada being relegated to the status of a "branch plant society" within the American order. Now, more than fifty years later, not only is it true that Canada is more firmly entrenched as a member of the American order as its

---

[2] The author is writing in 2019. The next federal election is expected to take place in October 2019.
[3] With a respectively wide safety-net of course.

reason for existing, it is becoming more evident that the liberal order is being seriously challenged to the point where an existential crisis is looming for all societies who have taken for granted the existence of our liberal-democratic societies and the material comforts which result from them.

Those who have been enriched by the comforts of the Western liberal order have long since dispensed of the historical relics of nation, tradition, and religion which they believe held humanity back for so long. The march of time is expressed by the progression of societies towards a more liberal state. Canada serves as a role model of what the liberal order sought to create: a society both wealthy and healthy with a political arena distinct for its moderate tone. It is undeniable that Canadians are quite content with their position in the liberal order despite what those lamenters may say. To lament for Canada because of its increasing reliance on American markets and the inevitable Americanization of Canada which follows from a deeper acceptance of American culture misses the point. Canada, America, and all other liberal-democracies are destined to homogenize in culture and politics since they are all expressions of an ideology which sees itself as the only legitimate form of human government. The historical traumas of the 20th century have convinced Western populations that any deviation from the post-war liberal ideology will inevitably lead to totalitarian atrocities and war. With the shadow of the 20th century still hanging over the West the liberal-democratic governments, along with leading intellectuals and public figures, have taken advantage of the given circumstances and exploited the traumas of that century in order to promote their views and convince their populations to accept "progress" as defined by a managerial elite.

What will happen to Canada in the years to come? Did George Grant lament too early? How will Canadians react when historical forces beyond their control or comprehension begin to bear down on the nation and force Canada out of its ideological slumber? What happens on the day when circumstances believed to be eternally consistent crumble at the slightest application of pressure from powers who do not take for granted the status quo? After all what future is there for a "post-national" state other than bureaucratic expansion and the inevitable loss of sovereignty to more powerful states? The continental destiny of Canada is the logical conclusion of not only Canada's run as a nation state but the whole idea of the nation state, at least in the Western world. As technology advances to the point where travel and communication is becoming almost instantaneous and unhindered by political and economic control or boundaries man will finally solve the issue of extending his domain over wide swaths of land by transcending time and space in order to impose his will where possible.

Canada can no longer ignore its geopolitical reality. Gone are the days when the Great White North could remain aloof in its North American cubby-hole, only addressing the world when it felt compelled to lecture others on the virtues of liberalism and its definition of justice. The next era of human history is going to see a struggle for hegemony over the world order and this means that all countries in every corner of the world will be at play. The continental destiny of Canada is more than just a matter of economic arrangements to promote trade with America and Mexico; Canada's continental destiny is ultimately securing the North American continent from attempts to undermine its cohesion and capabilities in projecting power in the world in its attempt to preserve the liberal world order. The Canada-America relationship is and has always been more than just a relationship of convenience it is a relationship of reciprocal necessity.

Canada is to America what the Roman provinces were; the vital parts of a system that needs to expand and harden in order to preserve the hegemony of the power at its centre. When the system remained intact all prospered and flourished; when the system collapsed the parts were left in a state of disbelief that a former golden age had come and passed and the days to come would be too horrible and alien to imagine. With Rome and its influence gone as a power the world it had created dissolved into a continent of warring peoples who were forced to fight for their existence as human beings. To quote Thucydides, "the strong did what they wanted and the weak suffered what they had to." If the world order that centers around America, an order which a large portion of the world has invested heavily in over the last eight decades, were to come to an end Canada, along with the rest, would be left to sink or swim in a world where the strong will once again do what they want the weak will be swept aside and reformed into parts of a new order.

This short book is little more than an observation of Canada and its world view from the point of view of someone who considers the taking for granted that progress in history a naïve view to hold at best and a dangerous delusion at worst. When a hegemonic system, one that has dissolved unique national cultures and homogenized into a single way of life, crumbles those rump states and remnant communities that remain will find that falling back on cultures that have long been given up as antiquated and colloquial will not be an option for those who so eagerly discarded what characterized what was once the expression of a unique historical experience of a unique historical state. The coming era of struggle will see the so-called post-war era come to a halt and begin again the process of reshaping systems that have reached the ends of their development.

The Election Year

The federal election of 2019[4] will come and go just as all the others have over the last fifteen decades of Canada's history as a nation state since confederation. Millions of Canadians will get the chance to cast their ballots and supposedly make a statement about the direction they want the country to go in. For some the election will be about the economy for others it will be education. Healthcare is always an important topic for elections. But two topics in particular will likely garner special attention this time around, immigration rates and carbon pricing to address climate change. These issues are where the leaders of the federal parties want the public to focus and it is there that the party platforms will be planted. What comes out of the next federal election will be yet another declaration by the people, the citizens, who in our liberal-democracy are sovereign.

For most Canadians the election issues we have briefly outlined above pretty much sum up what Canadian politics has become. Canadian politics reflects Canada as a whole; Canada is a liberal-democracy with a free market economy accompanied by an extensive social welfare structure. The division of powers between the federal government and provinces requires a certain amount of collaboration between politicians in order to fulfil the

---

[4] The author edited the present edition after the 2019 Federal election.

obligations the state has to its citizens. Provincial Premiers must consider their actions in light of what sort of assistance is available or can be expected from the federal government, be it in the form of federal funding of provincial programs or the altering of inter-provincial arrangements. Canadians have come to expect that their governments must always work in their favor to the exclusion of all other interests. The government of Canada is both servant to and protector of the Canadian public.

Why does writing any of this matter? Is it not self evident that a democratic government is by its very nature controlled and directed by the will of its people? Is anyone seriously questioning the importance of the democratic process? Of course Canadians are going to make an important decision on election day; by casting their ballots in support of one party over another the people are passing judgment on the policies and leadership of politicians. Of course it matters to the people which party is chosen to be allowed to implement its set of policy promises. No one can deny that the policies of certain political parties will impact the daily lives of Canadians by means of increased cost of living, employment opportunities, and quality of infrastructure and public services. But despite all the rhetoric being tossed about by such and such a politician the election *will not* reshape Canada's national destiny. Canada's liberal-democratic character is in no way in doubt. All that is being considered is how Canada's wealth will be harvested, what tax rates and schemes will be implemented, and where it will be shipped to, what programs it will be funneled to and at what rate. The election is not a life and death struggle the outcome of which will profoundly alter the fabric of Canadian society or it way of life. At its core the results will determine who the target of the public's ire will be for the next parliamentary term.

The reader may have noticed that we have seemingly overlooked one election issue that usually gets at the very least a passing glance and sometimes an honorable mention, Canada's foreign policy. A country's foreign policy is not just about international relations, it is more than economics and markets. A country's foreign policy is an expression of how a country views itself and how it wants other countries to view it. Despite what Canadians may want to believe Canada's foreign policy paints a picture of a country that is thoroughly entrenched as a member of the American international order. For all that it is worth the habit of successive Canadian governments to insist that Canada is a member of the "community of nations" and has a reputation of "peacekeeping" seems to fall flat when considering the impact Canada actually has in the world.

Since its establishment as a confederation of provinces back in 1867 Canada has played two distinct roles with regards to international relations: partner and subject. In the minds of most Canadians it is taken for granted that the *Dominion of Canada* is an independent and sovereign nation state that enjoys the respect of its allies and a high level of global prestige in matters of promoting liberalism and humanitarianism. Without a doubt the reader should assume that the role of Canada as a "peacekeeper" will be brought up over the course of the next election. The Liberal party will boast that *they* have brought Canada back to its role as an upholder of UN mandates. The Conservative party will say that in order to be a peacekeeper there must in the first place be an actual "peace" to keep. From a certain point of view each party is right. Canada has previously conducted peacekeeping missions but to say that Canada is *exclusively* a peacekeeper on the world stage is misleading. Alternatively peacekeeping missions may sometimes be an opportunity to assist NATO allies in an indirect way when Canada needs to "help out while not helping out." Nonetheless foreign policy is not a serious political issue for Canadians because Canada's place in the world and the role it plays was decided for it decades ago following the end of the Second World War.

The election year of 2019, for most Canadians, will change nothing in the way in which Canadians view themselves or their nation. And why should they do otherwise? There are those who thunder that since 2019 is an election year that this somehow signals great changes in the direction Canada is going to take in both foreign and domestic issues. What may some of these changes actually be? Will Canada make adjustments to its military alliances with America and NATO in order to start a strategic relationship with China or Russia? Will Canada become a rival to America for hegemony over North America or the Western hemisphere? Will Canada disengage from all military operations in the world including UN "peacekeeping" missions? On the domestic front is Canada suddenly going to transform itself into a federal republic, or will it suddenly disintegrate into a number of independent states[5]? Is Canada suddenly going to close its borders and disallow all migration into its territory? Is the Canadian government going to suddenly grant national autonomy to all indigenous peoples in Canada allowing for self-rule in large swaths of territory across Canada[6]? Is Canada going to suddenly dissolve its public health service system and replace it with a "laissez faire" market health system? Is the Canadian government going to suddenly nationalize all sectors of industry and declare public ownership of all capital produced? It does not seem likely that Canada would suddenly take such a

---

[5] Following the federal election in October 2019 a political movement called "Wexit" has sprung up calling for Ottawa to give greater attention to the Western provinces. The movement does not constitute a serious separatist threat to Canada.
[6] January 2020 saw a wave of protests by Indigenous rights groups making demands for greater autonomy. The protests lasted about a month and ended following negotiations between Indigenous leaders and Ottawa. In the end some concessions were granted to certain Indigenous tribes who claim territories along the route of natural gas pipeline projects. Despite what activists may wish to be the case this incident is not the first nor will it be the last time that Indigenous tribes use protests to gain benefits from Ottawa; demonstrations are simply a tool to gain financial concessions.

sharp political turn away from its historical experience all because of a single election.

Despite how much it may disappoint those who would like to see some of the above mentioned developments come to fruition, it is highly unlikely that such things will happen in the span of a single election cycle or government mandate. Like most other liberal democracies quick and sharp changes in policy do not come about through elections. Although in 2018 a number of provincial elections have been described as being "revolutionary" or "populist" in nature or that they represent a sharp departure from the norm, substantive differences in governance between one regime and the next has not lived up to the political or media hype. In Ontario Premier Ford stormed into office with the cheers of "the people" and the outcry of "the resistance." Ford was at once celebrated as a populist hero who won a majority mandate to reduce government overspending and at the same time condemned as a dangerous demagogue who plans to take Ontario back to the 1950's. After a year in office it cannot be said that Ford is living up to the "revolutionary" title like a Castro or a Lenin; although the opposition has been working exceptionally hard to frame every step Mr. Ford takes as earth shattering and a threat to the very fabric of Ontarian society business goes on as it did in the previous government. Despite what supporters of Mr. Ford may like to believe Ontario remains the most expensive province to live in with infrastructure unable to support the massive increase in the province's population;

and before opponents of Mr. Ford can begin celebrating they must face the fact that since taking office the province has not been thrown into disarray or taken back fifty years. Premier Ford is not a "king" or a "dictator," he is merely a career politician managing a large bureaucracy.

The other "populist revolution" to sweep through provincial politics was in Quebec. In October of 2018 the people of Quebec cast their ballots to elect a new premier and a new ruling party. Just like in Ontario the media would have the public believe that the end times were upon us and that a wave of political radicalism would spread across the province. Instead, what *did* result from the election was the coming to power of Francois Legault, a moderately conservative businessman-turned-politician who ran on promises of tax reforms and the continued secularization of public institutions and Quebec society in general. The once formidable separatist movement of Quebec seems to have finally been laid to rest, at least for the next political generation, and those francophone Canadians who are not completely satisfied with Ottawa seem to have settled for a policy of wringing out concessions from the Federal government to make life inside confederation just a bit more comfortable for Quebecers[7].

---

[7] The 2019 federal election saw the Bloc Québécois rise to the position of third party. The reader must keep in mind that the Bloc Québécois of 2019 is not separatist in nature but is instead a pressure group that advocates for greater Quebec autonomy

These are only two examples and do not necessarily prove our thesis[8]. But the portrayal of these elections by certain politicians and those in the media is enough to convince neurotic political-wonks in the population that there has been some sort of fundamental change in Canadian society and these elections are proof positive.

This author insists that there has *not* been a fundamental change in Canadian politics and that this is because there has been no reason, be it historical or economic development, which demands a fundamental change. Despite what events have gone on in the rest of the world Canadian society seldom feels the effects of most overseas political movements or wars, and when it does it is limited to those who are directly involved in those events or through their families. But as far as Canada goes it remains firmly fixed along its path towards some idealized future promised to it by the dominant political ideology in the West, democratic liberalism. This is not to say that Canada is immune to the social and political forces sweeping other parts of the world, it only

---

within Confederation. The party may be described as an advocate of Quebec interests and a negotiating agent in Ottawa.

[8] Since this work's initial writing there has been another political upset in provincial politics. In Alberta Jason Kenny and his United Conservative Party won a majority mandate. This can hardly be regarded as a political revolution especially given Alberta's political history of seeing strong conservative support on both the federal and provincial levels. The election results in Prince Edward Island and Newfoundland and Labrador are further testament to the stability in Canadian politics.

means that the blessings of geography have insulated Canada from the harshness of the new great game developing brought on by the weakening of liberal internationalism. But this insulation will quickly erode away in the event of a catastrophic collapse of the international order which American hegemony has created.

The Ideology

With 2019 being an election year in Canada it is only natural that political "wonks" and gossipers will be looking to the "diviners of public opinion" for insider information, and they will wait with bated breath as the crystal ball of "the polls" is consulted. It is considered sound practice to consider provincial elections as a sort of temperature taking in order to get a feeling of the political mood of the country. If 2018 was any indication of things to come then we are likely safe in our expectations that despite all the fear mongering and declaring a political revolution on the horizon that Canadians will once again reinforce their support for the system while only demanding small concessions along the lines of lowering the cost of living or increases in public services.

The fact that is not immediately grasped by the many who dabble in political commentaries and the espousing of opinions is that the nature of the Canadian political system is shaped by the ideology that serves as its spirit and inspiration, liberalism. Despite having a tradition dating back several hundred years, liberalism is still wrongly associated with particular political parties or positions on the political spectrum. The ideology of liberalism cannot be said to be inherently left or right just as it cannot solely be used as a label for those who follow a specific political party. Once we understand that Canada is inherently liberal in nature then it becomes clear why it is not reasonable to expect sharp and violent deviations of Canada's political course as long as its liberal heritage remains strong.

The term "liberal" has been used by some on the right of the political spectrum to paint all left leaning political parties in a certain way, often dismissing political platforms in their entirety. Those parties labeled "liberal" are commonly described as being politically "progressive" and secular in their views, they are also sometimes described as leaning towards social-democracy; both definitions painting similar pictures of outcomes for societies traveling down such paths. Although this may be an accurate way to describe certain parties the general use of the term "liberal" is much too misleading and a-historical when we consider the origin and development of the political movement known to us as "liberalism." By "liberalism" we mean the political ideology explored and explained by such thinkers as Hobbes, Locke, Mill, Rousseau, Smith, Popper, Pierre Trudeau and any other thinkers who take as his or her political focal point the individual and *his* relation to political structures[9]. Liberalism treats political institutions as being created for

---

[9] I say "political structures" rather than only "the state" because there are certain branches of the liberal school of thought that breaks down "states" into a number of loosely associated institutions that the individual may or may not interact with. For example liberal legal theorists will explore the individual's relation to specific legal institutions such as a court of law or law enforcement without considering at all other notions such as citizenship and the social contract.

the sole reason of providing an environment suitable for the free and safe enjoyment of individual life. More contemporary trends in the liberal school of thought which stem from *Modernity* tend to hone in on the "middle-class" way of live as being the ideal expression of liberalism and the standard by which government actions are to be measured by[10]. "Economic man" and his daily concerns equal the sum total of political science and the logical product of political history.

The central tenets of liberalism are usually understood as the supremacy of the individual over the collective, materialism, economic or "rational" organizing of material, universal human rights, and representative democracy accompanied and sustained by the rule of law. This is not an exhaustive list of core beliefs of the liberal school of thought and does not necessarily explain how such beliefs are translated into political action. For example, what constitutes representative democracy is sometimes envisioned as being based on simple majority rule while at other times it is expressed as proportional representation; democratic rule is qualified by the extent to which elections actually express the will of the population or a significant minority within the population. Another tenant of liberalism that is without consensus of its actual meaning is the meaning of "supremacy of the individual." The limit of the rights of the individual in

---

[10] Philosophically liberalism equates middle class living with "the good life."

relation to the state and other individuals is something that causes serious divisions among political parties in *any* liberal democracy. How much "agency" does the individual have a right to and what is the role, if any, of the state to mediate between individuals? How much responsibility does the individual have when asked to face the consequences of his or her actions without society intervening? Does society have an obligation to mitigate perceived injustices allegedly originating from "systemic" beliefs caused by the organizing of a society?

One aspect of liberalism which is not only disagreed upon by liberals but is also one that most liberals would rather overlook than have to understand (and admit to) its implications on societies is predominance of materialism in the liberal world view. The materialist nature of liberalism stems from liberalism's focus on the individual and his own comforts while setting aside other matters such as the "common good" or group interests as metaphysical and unimportant to liberal political science. Materialism for liberals is the inevitable product left over when human societies are stripped of such aspects which may have a limiting or defining effect on the individual and his rights; concepts forming group identity such as history, religion, language, tradition, and national identity are all aspects of human society that have been attacked or "deconstructed" for putting some "collective" before the individual or for not considering the material and economic wellbeing of certain members of a society. Of course it may be said that the individual may choose freely what he or she wishes to associate as or with, be it a particular religion or culture; but this inevitably leads one to ask the question "if association with factors such as history, religion, and tradition, not to mention the new boutique identities of sexual and gender expression, is essentially elastic and determined by personal preference then what is left for organized society to provide to the individual?" If organized society and the institutions which humans create to administer laws and promote norms is expected to remain silent in shaping the character and identity of the individual then what is left for it to do? This question is answered by the fundamentals of materialism. Materialism focuses on the management of goods and their use in an environment in order to arrange them in such a way as to fulfill not only basic human needs like food, shelter, and clothing but also to allow for the free expression of human desires like comfort seeking, entertainment and ease of living. The individualistic nature of liberalism requires that the management of material goods be given top priority by the state in order to fulfill its political purpose of providing individuals with the necessities which are conducive to safe, secure, comfortable, and free lives where personal liberties and rights are given their maximum range to grow. In this light it should come as no surprise that liberal-democracies have been tightly married to capitalism by way of free markets; after all, where else can the personal tastes and appetites of masses of "individuals" be satisfied without too much restriction?

In its historical context liberalism developed out of historical developments in European societies where a growing political consciousness was coinciding with the development of the nation state. The beginning of the nation state gave rise to a new entity through which people could express their identities. With language serving as its underlying basis the nation state would go on to define its purpose as being the promotion of its people and their "common wealth." Whether in the form of a republic or monarchy the nation state became, at least superficially, an expression of popular will. Liberalism's place in the history of the nation state was the role it played in codifying and institutionalizing aspects of its ideology in relation to the evolving mechanisms of the state. Constitutions, parliaments, the separation of powers, law courts, common law, the rights of man, industrial and technological developments, and commercial law all resulted from liberalism taking effective control of the nation state as the leading ideology. Those who advocated for liberalism to be the dominant state ideology argued that the results of increased liberties would undeniably increase the power and wealth of the state by means of economic activity and an increased level of social happiness. As states began to gather wealth it was inevitable that those who made up society and saw themselves as generating the wealth began to demand a greater say in the political decision making process. What came of this demand for greater political consideration was an overall transformation of Western society from being dominated by distinctions of nobility and traditionalism to commercialism and leaders of technological innovation. The move away from "the old" and towards "the new" is a fundamental element of liberalism and is important to understand when trying to make sense of its historical developments.

The social contract stands as the central pillar of the modern state and it is from it that governments must now obtain their legitimacy from. If the state is to benefit from the fruits of its subjects then it is going to have to repay the favor by providing the necessities to life, liberty, and security of the person[11]. As with all aspects of human society concepts and institutions are constantly subject to the marching of history which does not leave them in the same state for very long.

Liberalism, including its various branches on both the left and right of the political spectrum, has developed into an understanding of the purpose of human society that sees the social contract as being less a reciprocal relationship of duties between the citizen and the state but instead rewrites the "contract" as a declaration of rights and benefits that individuals can expect to have granted to

---

[11] It must be stressed that providing the necessities for liberty is not the same as providing services or benefits. All that is meant by necessities are those certain arrangements which make possible certain activities and living standards. This distinction and the disagreements stemming from defining it plays a central role in the contemporary debate over the meaning of liberalism and its roles and limits.

them by a welfare state. This new expression of liberalism which was popularized around the middle of the 20th century is the guiding principle of all political parties in Canada with the only difference being where each party views the ideal limits of individual expectations.

The fundamental difference between the varying trends in the liberal ideology is the question to what degree the individual is granted the freedom to choose what he deems "good" when considering how his or her choices and tastes impact the freedoms of other individuals who are equally free to determine their own tastes; the boundary between "private" and "public" affairs is what commonly determines one's association with either being to the left or the right on the political spectrum in liberal democracies. When it comes to the political parties found across Canada this difference in degree of personal autonomy is the only real distinguishing factor.

The political parties of Canada are all fundamentally liberal in their ideology and world view. All consider the preservation of individual rights, the separation of "private" and "public" matters, and the managing of material as the central role that the state should play in the lives of its population.

But if all the political parties of Canada are so similar in nature then one is faced with a dilemma, "which party is right for me?" This question is not an easy one to answer especially if what we have said above has any truth to it; if liberalism is the ideology shared by all political parties then how is it that there have come to be multiple parties? The fact that the various dominant parties of Canada are all expressions of liberalism is evidence that the Canadian world view is firmly established and the political environment has been thoroughly pacified.

Perhaps the reader will recoil at the term we are to use to describe the role in society that the political parties compete for control over. The outcome of any election held in any part of Canada, and most places in the modern West, determines which party of the varying forms of liberalism is going to be allowed to *engineer* society for its own end; the end being the promotion and preservation of political power. The term *engineering* may strike some as an odd and even ominous word choice to describe the governance process. But to say that politics is the *engineering* of society is appropriate in order to really grasp what it means to govern a society like Canada. Canada and its geopolitical situation requires not only steady and predictable governance but also a conscious acceptance of circumstances dictating the necessity to act in such ways as to preserve the accepted ideology of Canada and by extension the Western world.

"But we live in a free society which emphasises individual rights; governments do not *engineer* liberty and happiness, rather, people live as they see fit." It is true that Canada is a free and open society. Its adherence to liberal ideology has resulted in political and legal institutions which defend and nurture individual rights and its economic system emphasises individual tastes and preferences while accepting that there are certain expectations when it comes to economic activity. All of this does not come about on its own accord. The institutions which make up Canada are more than just a superficial expression of the social contract; they go further in shaping the very character of the society from which they were established in the first place. If Canada is a liberal-democracy valuing individual rights it is because it has been designed to function in order to be such. As a modern state the workings of Canadian governance are not as simple as "vote and execute." There is a continuous dialectical relationship between the governed and the governing which necessarily results in the continuous existence of Canada as a liberal state. If liberalism means individual rights, materialism, political representation, and supremacy of the individual then it is the obligation of those who demand liberalism and those who implement it to ensure the necessary elements are present in order for it to be sustained. In order to sustain a liberal order it is necessary to have both its domestic and foreign requirements satisfied. Canada enjoys the necessities of favorable governance in abundant amounts; geopolitically Canada is secure due to its geography and close affiliation with the United States, and domestically Canada is not faced with any existential crisis which could seriously challenge or disrupt its institutions. Because of its favorable circumstances Canada is able to function as its deeply held ideology dictates.

In short, Canada has been engineered as a market based consumer society where the only acceptable political expression is in the form of what liberal-democratic ideology deems so. Culture in Canada is whatever market forces and liberal ideology deem permissible; particularly that it does not cause disruption to the historical development of the liberal-democratic state.

It is not our intention to provide a comprehensive discussion of liberalism but only provide the reader with a general picture of the ideology in order to understand its nature and how it shapes Canadian society. Since the 19th century liberalism has dominated Western political arenas inspiring political movements around the world all with a common goal of bringing about liberal-democracy as the ruling ideology. Canada has long been at the forefront of the movement not only domestically but on the international stage: first as a faithful colony to the British Empire and then as a close ally to America. Just as with all societies in the world Canada's history is what has shaped its character and produced the liberal-democracy it is today. Once this is understood it is then possible to understand why Canada's very existence begins and ends with international liberalism and why it would be suicidal for Canadian society to fundamentally break with its current trajectory.

The Election

This brings us to the purpose of Canada's electoral system. If Canada is to be regarded as a liberal-democracy then it is expected that there must be some sort of democratic electoral process. But what is actually achieved by the electoral process and what bearing does it have on Canada as a nation? Is it nothing more than choosing between "blue," "red," or "orange?" Is it just a popularity contest? Ultimately is it actually a democratic expression of Canada's citizenry and its destiny?

If we take the time to consider the political programs put forward by Canada's main political parties it is clear that none of the parties find the political situation in Canada to be *so* unacceptable as to warrant revolutionary and fundamental changes to Canadian political, economic, legal, or social institutions.

Despite the rhetoric which is likely to be used over the next year the stakes in the election will be no higher than those of past elections. This is not to say that the consequences of the next election or any other election are irrelevant. There are real issues being fought over which will impact the lives of millions of Canadians in different ways. But to say that the election of a particular party or the forming or a particular government marks a tremendous shift in Canadian history is nothing but hyperbole.

What are the stakes in this election? What are the issues highlighting this next round in the political arena? While the reader may have a list of issues he or she regards as important it must be admitted that not all issues are going to be given the same value by all Canadians. Therefore I admit that the list of issues that follows is not exhaustive and is not meant to be so. My intention is to provide a taste of the kinds of issues that liberal-democratic societies regard as both consequential and within the power of the democratic process to "solve."

One issue on the table is the introduction of a federal carbon tax in order to address issues stemming from climate change. In one corner of the political arena we have the Liberals who plan to introduce a "price on emissions/carbon" to curb greenhouse gases which cause pollution and lead to climate change as well as generate tax revenue and invest it in future technologies and fuels. In the other corner of the political arena we have the Conservatives promising to "scrap the carbon tax" in order to protect jobs and who also promise to introduce "effective means" of combating climate change while allowing the economy to grow. There are two points made by each side of the debate: the pro-carbon tax side claims that it is necessary to introduce a price on carbon emissions in order to bring down Canada's carbon emissions to meet its global commitments and secondly it is said that the revenue generated through pricing provides much needed investments to promote green energy projects and technologies in order to prepare Canada for the future "green economy." Those opposed express concern that firstly the tax will not actually reduce emissions and secondly it will hinder Canadian business and damage Canada's economy by slowing down economic growth.

However unclear the outcome of either side's plans may be what is clear is that as the trends of technology and economics go so too will Canada be dragged in that direction. If in fact there is no carbon tax implemented this does not necessarily mean that the cost of living will go down, at least not in the long run. The trend in the West seems to be an ever increasing cost of living no matter the political policies implemented. Also if no carbon tax is implemented this does not guarantee future growth for Canadian industry because as business has no national loyalties or sentimentality for social consequences beyond profits if companies calculate that downsizing or relocating is in their interest then they will do so despite the protests, or begging, by politicians. Alternatively the implementation of a carbon tax does not necessarily translate into a reduction of emissions, for as long as there are profits to be made and demands for more products from consumers then the annoyances of a tax will not stand in the way of satisfying the demands of a population of consumers[12]. And let it be said that the collection of any

---

[12] Isn't it ironic how no politician will dare to put forward ideas of self-control, moderation, and frugality as ways of combating the detrimental effects to the environment that hyper consumerist manufacturing and consumption has? One suspects

tax revenues in no way guarantees *effective* use of said revenue for investments into "green energy" technologies or projects or that any of the so called projects will produce worthwhile returns. A tax is a tax and there is nothing more addictive to government than the immediate revenue generated from a tax. Parties on the left and right are highly susceptible to the addictive nature of taxation.

Election season inevitably includes a discussion of Canada's foreign policy and imagined role in the world. There will be much rhetorical talk of Canada's reputation and image being at stake; if such and such a party takes power then Canada will lose its reputation of "peacemaking" and engagement or if another party takes power then Canada's foreign policy will take a nationalist turn inwards. Elections are always a time for Canadians to reminisce about their history of peacekeeping missions. While Canadians like to think of themselves as good peacekeepers they tend to overlook the role Canada plays in upholding not just UN customs and laws but also preserving the American led liberal-democratic world order. Foreign policy inevitably includes military policy. Whatever Canadians think that peacekeeping means Canada is going to be deploying armed *lethal* force against other countries and non-state actors. Nonetheless most Canadians can afford to live totally oblivious to the realities of international relations.

---

that it would be political suicide to preach the virtues of being content with less. Let not the frugal run for office.

In the election of 2015 there were a number of heated exchanges between then Prime Minister Stephen Harper and Liberal party leader Justin Trudeau over Canada's role in the ongoing war against the Islamic State of Iraq and Syria. When the Islamic State stormed onto the world stage in the summer of 2014 after launching its invasion of Northern-Iraq from their base territory in Eastern Syria the world media went into a panic. Report after report about the atrocities being committed by this seemingly invincible army of jihadists stressed the need for international reaction to stop this monstrous force. During that same summer the United States began an air campaign against the Islamic State, striking their forces in Northern Iraq. Shortly thereafter a coalition was formed in order to combat the Islamic State[13]. Canada played an important role in the campaign by providing hundreds of soldiers and, initially, fighter aircraft. During the election in 2015 Canada's role in the campaign against the Islamic State was brought into question by both the Liberals and NDP who engaged in criticising Prime Minister Harper's decision to take a combat role in the campaign[14]. Despite

---

[13] American operations against ISIS were given the name Operation Inherent Resolve. Shortly after operations began American formed the Combined Joint Task Force to organize international efforts against ISIS.

[14] While claiming to support a campaign against ISIS Trudeau criticised Canada's air campaign as nothing more than a chance for Prime Minister Harper "to whip out our CF-18s and show them how big they are." The flippant remark was repeated in Canadian media all the way up to the 2015 general election.

being a vocal critic of Canada's combat role in Iraq and Syria, after winning the election with a majority and announcing that he was ending Canada's air campaign against ISIS the newly elected Prime Minister Trudeau continued to commit Canadian troops and equipment to the war effort. Canada remained a member of the anti-ISIS coalition through Prime Minister Trudeau's first term in office and has committed Canada's involvement in the regional campaign into the future past the 2019 election.

This is not the only time Canada has played a combat role in recent years. In 2011 the NATO coalition launched a military intervention in Libya during that country's civil war in order to, as was claimed at the time, execute a UN resolution implementing a no-fly zone over the country. What resulted from the intervention into the ongoing civil war was an overthrowing of the long time leader Colonel Gaddafi followed by the collapse of the Libyan state and any notion of a central authority in the country. In this and the above mentioned campaigns Canada's justifications for joining in the American led coalitions was "humanitarian intervention" and upholding of international law. Whatever one thinks of the validity of Canada's excuse for joining American led military campaigns, or whether Canada has an *obligation* to get involved, the overall geopolitical consequences tend to speak louder than any liberal "good intentions" or claims to only be concerned with human rights and not calculations of power on a global scale. It goes without saying that whether or not Canada is wearing the patch of an international coalition or a United Nations peacekeeping mission Canada seems always to be working towards the interests of its traditional NATO allies. It seems that whatever promises are made during political campaigns the outcome is the same no matter what party takes control. It has to be assumed that the parties of Canada are aware of the attitude amongst many Canadians of being staunchly, even stubbornly, against war. This is why the parties are careful to balance public perception with security commitments; Canada only involves itself in "just wars" based on humanitarian grounds and it is imperative that these wars are framed as such despite the actual developments on the ground.

Immigration will be another topic greeted with heated rhetoric but with little actual political consequences. It must be firmly stated that none of the major parties of Canada are against immigration. Each of the big three parties, Liberal, Conservative, and NDP, are in favor of continuing Canada's tradition of welcoming in immigrants not only as a gesture of liberal good-will but also keeping up with economic and demographic demands. Unfortunately the predictable development of the next campaign will be that certain parties will accuse one party in particular as being "racist" and "anti-immigrant." The Conservative party of Canada is going to be raked over the coals by the Liberals and NDP on immigration no matter what policies are actually suggested by Andrew Scheer.

It has become a pitiful scene over the last number of years watching members of the Conservative party again and again have to make public statements about their deep love and support for immigration to Canada and being followed up by a frenzy of condemnation, and rightly so, of racists and "white supremacists." But no matter how many times the Conservatives state the fact that they are not an anti-immigration party and no matter what pro-immigration policies they implement when in office it is still politically effective for the Liberals and NDP to *accuse* the Conservatives of harboring racist intentions or beliefs. Why is this so? Why is labeling right leaning political parties as racist such an easy tactic? It is because political rhetoric since the end of the Second World War has come to associate "right-wing politics" to bigotry. Inherent in the conservative ideology[15] is the belief that

---

[15] That is "small 'c' conservative" rather than the Conservative Party of Canada. The same goes for our use of the term "liberal," that is "small 'l' liberal" rather than Liberal Party of Canada. As has been noted in a previous chapter both the major parties of Canada are "liberal" in that they have their roots in the liberal ideology that came out of the 19th century; an ideology promoting individual liberties and rights over collective interests. At the beginning of the 21st century many ask the question whether or not developments over the 20th century have fundamentally severed contemporary liberalism's roots. Although members of certain social sciences would say that the roots *have* been severed due to social and political movements over the last century the author however does not agree with this view and insists that liberalism as expressed in the 21st century retains enough of its ties to earlier developments that it would be wrong to declare it to be something different entirely. But this

law and order is necessary to counteract the passion and violence of human nature especially when it is in the form of a mob of uninformed voters. Perhaps Edmund Burke explained it best by describing what happens when human nature is "liberated" from its former social and legal constraints. When human nature is freed from the constraints put on it by human society, such as laws and customs, it is natural that there will be a dash towards the most extreme displays of base human desires and violence; the ability of demagogues to wield the masses for political purposes has been repeated throughout history. Burke and other conservative thinkers like him stress that if a well organized human society is to function then it is necessary for organized society to place on men and women certain constraints such as laws and social norms. This does not mean that humans are to be oppressed or "yoked" by the law. It means that if one realistically expects the social contract to function as intended then there must be rules and borders aimed at maintaining the stability of society and the free and secure enjoyment of one's own life. This is a core belief that gives rise to many of the policies and views expressed by conservative parties in the West; liberty must be accompanied by responsibility.

The Conservative party of Canada is no exemption to the long tradition of conservative thought despite its

---

does not mean that liberalism has remained totally unchanged over the centuries; this would be a-historical.

distinctly "Canadian" nature. These conservative roots are what parties and thinkers of the left are fundamentally set against; structures of society are looked at with extreme suspicion by those on the left. Despite what is believed or admitted to by opponents of the Conservatives the Conservative party of Canada is in fact a liberal party. If we consider what we have said above about liberalism then it is obvious that the Conservatives, Liberals, *and even* NDP[16] are liberal at their core and vary in their particular branch of liberalism. This being said the major difference between left and right wing parties in the vein of liberal-democracy is their respective approach to preserving or reforming pillars of democratic society; reform does not mean revolution and preservation does not mean regression.

Coming back to the question of immigration policy in Canada each of the three parties mentioned support

---

[16] The NDP espouses policies which could be construed as being socialistic but it still remains thoroughly embedded in liberal ideology. It is hard to see how the NPD's platform of building extensive government bureaucracies and an expanded social welfare system could be implemented without a steep increase of taxation on existing wealth which is euphemistically called "redistribution of wealth." The NDP is very careful in trying to ease fears that arise when socialist terms like "redistribution" are used; as a "social-democratic" party the NDP believes in promoting individual rights by providing more comforts and opportunities to more people at the expense of "the haves." The fiery and revolutionary rhetoric has been toned down in the party's program to the point that many ask why the NDP does not just merge with the Liberal party.

Canada's current immigration policies of openness and acceptance of peoples from all corners of the world. There are only minor differences in the policies each party promises to implement if only they were in a position to do so. These differences include the language used to describe certain details and what details are focused on. The Liberals have taken it upon themselves to become the party of "saving refugees" and have tried to shift the thinking of immigration away from people simply moving to Canada seeking a better life and opportunities to a view of seeing Canada "saving" those coming to the country; Canada is duty bound to "save" the world from itself by providing asylum to all those who seek it. The Conservatives also admit that Canada does in fact play an important role in welcoming refugees from the most dangerous places in the world. The previous Conservative government headed by Prime Minister Harper was a vocal supporter of rescuing Christian minorities in the Middle-East and Yazidis who were fleeing from the advancing armies of the Islamic State. The opposition at the time criticized the government's policies because it had identified *specific* at risk groups as eligible for making refugee claims. The Conservative government was accused of being too selective in its refugee policies. Those on the left were politically incapable of accepting that while it would be wonderful to provide aid to everyone it was not possible to move so quickly without social and political consequences. One needs only consider the situation in a number of Western European countries since welcoming in large numbers of asylum seekers in such a short amount of time. The Conservative party has seemingly learned that there are real consequences to allowing ideals dictate actions.

The NDP is hardly worth mentioning when it comes to immigration policies. Their policies are essentially the same as those of the Liberals only expressed using more "socialistic" rhetoric such as "no borders," and "no one is illegal."

To those who would point to the increasingly vocal anti-immigrant sentiment in Europe as proof that there is a growing strain of bigotry in the West it is necessary to remind them to keep historical context in mind when trying to understand events. The overall growth of "populist movements" on the side of the Euro-sceptics cannot be reduced to indigenous Europeans rejecting immigration. To say such a thing would be to first show a disdain for the concerns of the common people of Europe and secondly to give complete amnesty to those political and financial forces who have squandered the wealth of the continent and are trying to place the consequences on the European people. An unfortunate trend that has developed since the latter half of the previous century is the whittling-down of the public memory to the length and duration of a news cycle. After being whipped up into a frenzy by news stories filled with "recent developments" and saturated with "facts on the ground" and "expert analysis" it is amazing that the memory of these events fades shortly after the news cycle is restarted and a new story takes the headlines; those who boasted about being "up to date" with the facts and who "follow the news" are suddenly left in the dark when the next "breaking" story happens a quickly turn to the new hot take. Most people who "consume" news do so without critically considering the facts being put forward and how such facts are being presented; for whom are such and such facts benefitting? Worst of all most news watchers do not follow a story long enough to discover future developments which may dispute earlier conclusions.

Collective amnesia of historical events is a staple in our society of trends and cycles. The events following the 2008 financial crisis is a case in point. The financial crisis was not limited to the year 2008 nor was it limited to events in America. The entire world was jolted into a panic over the viability of a global financial system built solely on the economic wellbeing of a single power. If we shift out focus on Europe we find that the financial crisis threatened to bring down not only the financial institutions of the EU but the social welfare apparatus of each of the individual nation states. Political and financial leaders from across Europe scrambled to find solutions to the crisis and in the end decided to blame Europeans themselves for the crisis. It was by those in government and financial institutions that Europeans needed to "tighten their belts" and learn that there were "no fee lunches." Austerity became the name of the game and it would be implemented through a combination of political and banking coercion to force certain countries identified as being "too wasteful" with European money to "reform" to the standards set by Brussels. What followed was a period of civil unrest across the continent in the form of mass demonstrations against the unpopular austerity measures. Those who opposed austerity rejected the EU explanation of the financial crisis that blamed high national debt for the economic slowdown and subsequent unemployment rate increases. Instead, demonstrators pointed to the political and financial leaders and institutions of Europe as being responsible for mismanaging European economic matters and enriching themselves at the expense of the common good. To say that this period of European history is unrelated to the "populist movements" which emerged a few years later is a sign of an unbelievable ignorance of politics and the interconnection of events.

The growing discontent in Europe and instances of political violence there has been quickly turned into an opportunity to generate propaganda by a number of parties. For Canadian politicians and public figures to exploit the unrest in Europe for their own aims is not surprising. It is politically prudent to exploit events beneficial to one's own political position. The playing up of fears and resentment is a time honored way of swaying the masses into seeing things as one wishes them to see them and also of motivating those masses into taking some sort of action, usually by voting in a certain way. Just as those politically astute leaders in Europe have come to rely on the historical trauma of the 20th century to retain control over Europeans and restrain the political demands and expectations of the public so too do Canadian politicians and public figures prey upon the mild manners of Canadians by spreading fears of religious or political extremists or even hatred for specific countries in order to motivate policy initiatives such as cracking down on "misinformation" or "fighting terrorism."

Unlike what played out in the 2016 presidential election in the United States the "culture war" that waged there and still rages there will not play a major role in the next Canadian election. Although there are instances where Canadian historical heritage and culture is seemingly put under fire by those on the "progressive left" there is no serious movement in Canada which has the preservation of "traditional" Canadian culture as its core aim. But why is this so? When the Second World War ended there developed in the Western mind a phobia of things regarded as "belonging to the past." This was brought on by the real historical trauma experienced by Western society brought on by two suicidal world wars. Whether rightly or wrongly the popular explanation for why the wars broke out has been placed on some vague notions of "backwards thinking", native-ism, and radical traditionalism; those who were victorious in the end, including the United States and the Soviet Union, were granted the privilege of writing their own narratives as to why events played out as they did, ideology playing a major role in shaping the narrative. Since the end of the last world war political parties on both the left and right have found it politically prudent to play on the public fear of another war being possible and their desire to avoid another at all costs. For many countries, including those on the winning side, 1945 became their historical "year zero" where events which happened before did so because people lived in the age of ignorance while from 1945 onwards the march of progress would lift the world out from the ashes of history and into a new age; Americans preached their belief in the democratic future where every man would be free to choose to live his life as he pleased; Soviets preached the sermon of the coming of the age of the proletarian where the worker would once and for all be liberated from the shackles of his former capitalist exploiter. Both Americans and Soviets emphasised that only by looking forward could humanity achieve the desired future and that looking backwards only brought on feelings of regret and misery. The effects of historical trauma can be seen in examples of political rhetoric where policies are promoted as being the only way to avoid "the events of the 30's" or that certain foreign policies are a return to colonialism or isolationism. If a proposed policy was suspected of being "antiquated" then it was immediately attacked and discarded.

Canada, although spared the fires of war at home, twice answered the call of the British Empire to come to its aid in the face of its continental rivals, particularly Germany. After serving its imperial motherland so admirably Canada was left in an awkward spot as its recent role of defender of the Empire was left hollow when the British Empire finally exhausted itself as a world power and was forced to hand over the torch to the United States.

The impact of the World Wars was truly global in scope and nature. No society was left unchanged by the developments and outcome of the war. In order to cope with the historical trauma Western countries began to display a fanatical support for "progress" at the expense of their historical identities. The only acceptable ideology that "legitimate" parties were allowed to have was liberalism partnered with free market capitalism which marked the beginning of the new technological age.

Canada, like most Western countries, suffers from low historical self-esteem and displays a high confidence in the "goodness" of progressive idealism. The logical conclusion of its ideology has brought Canada to the point where the sitting Prime Minister[17] was able to say that Canada is a "post-national society" without the fear of a serious backlash or damage to his political standing. Perhaps he has a point. After all is it not the responsibility of the state to provide for the necessities of life, liberty, and individual security? Is not the "national" character of the nation state anathema to the ideology of liberalism once it is taken to its logical conclusion?

---

[17] Justin Trudeau was Prime Minister at the time of this writing.

Since taking power Prime Minister Trudeau has expressed his support for a sort of historical revisionism aimed at making contemporary society more "just" in light of Canada's perceived historical injustices. Rather than admiring Canada's history of European settlement in North America and the hardships that were overcome in order to forge a nation Canadians are reminded that North America was not an empty continent but was inhabited by indigenous peoples who were almost completely wiped out through wars, disease, and conquest at the hands of Europeans. Developments in social justice ideologies have resulted in the re-examination of history using a "critical lens." The realigning of historical narratives to be more in line with ideologies and sentiments of "the current year" has taken on much momentum in Western countries over the last few years and it was inevitable that Canada too would undergo the same process. This is what lies behind calls for the removal of statues of important political figures including Canada's first Prime Minister Sir John A. Macdonald. The response from the Conservative party of Canada has been a sort of lukewarm superficial regret over the apparent erasing of Canada's national history. But what has this expression of concern actually achieved? The public concern for the removal of statues and the "looking at history through a critical lens[18]" seems

---

[18] By "critical lens" it is commonly understood to mean an ideological view held by those to the left of the political spectrum including "social-justice" advocates and also by self identified "socialists" or "Marxists." However it would be wrong to say that it is completely motivated by actual ideology,

to evaporate quickly after the news coverage ends. It truly is a lamentable thing to watch when a country's history and culture is being erased and then long after it has been replaced to see a few citizens suddenly pay attention as though this is somehow a new development.

The culture war in Canada is superficial at best. It does not have to do with preserving traditional Canadian culture but rather the culture of commercialism and materialism which stems from liberalism and the cult of the individual. To say that "Canada is not what it used to be" is an understatement lost on those same people who claim that "immigrants and foreigners" are somehow changing Canadian culture. They shake their heads in dismay as restaurants with "weird" names open up or as television channels show people speaking another language while they are at the same time wallowing in their American made materialist culture where the cheapest fastest foods, the flashiest movies, and the hottest musical hits are to them the epitome of bliss. Who is Gordon Lightfoot when compared with Beyonce? McDonalds and Burger King and Taco Bell and Tim Horton's are all the nutrition needed besides the conveniently pre-packaged meal in a box. It is the cause of the local sports team that wins the hearts and minds of the

---

there must be room for scepticism as to the genuineness on the part of politicians, celebrities, and corporations who advocate for "social change" while retaining control of political and financial power. The social justice industry is very lucrative.

masses while expressions of "Canadiana" are scoffed at and ridiculed for their quaintness.

Whatever racial prejudices some may still hold such people have no legitimate right to assign blame for changing the culture of Canada to those who come from different racial, cultural, or religious backgrounds. The assignment of blame to "new Canadians" for being responsible for the changing face of society shows a complete lack of understanding of historical developments. What changes in society that can legitimately be attributed to immigration is nothing in comparison to the earth shattering changes imposed on Canadian society by American advanced-industrialism and commercialism brought on by the movement towards continentalism. The great Canadian "culture war" was lost decades before Canadians even began to get a sense that there was something funny going on.

It is hard to believe that the window dressing that is Canada's "link" to the British Crown could convince anyone that Canada is anything but an extension of American political, economic, and cultural power. The very notion of a "culture war" begins to ring quite hollow when one considers what it is that the warring sides are fighting over; an ultra-commercialized, technologically unrestrained, socially atomized, and hopelessly nihilistic wasteland of history, or in other words the "End of History." The next election will not be a victory in the "culture war" and it does not provide an opportunity to "take back our country." For as long as Canadians are content with the invasion of atomizing materialism then there is no legitimate right to claim that the country is being "stolen." Canada was bought out a long time ago, and the coinage used was technology, security, and plenty.

But Canada cannot be blamed for its enjoyment of material comforts any more than can any society who enjoys what it is culturally engineered to value. If liberalism is truly the dominant ideology of Canadian society then it must be the case that above all Canadians value the preference of the individual over the group, technological advances over antiquated methods, satisfaction and gratification over temperance and abstinence, the moment over the long view, subjective standards over objective values, economic prosperity over historical and cultural continuance, "sunny ways" over harsh realities, and idealism and what "ought to be" over realism and "what actually is."

Those who see the culture war as some sort of crusade to defend Canada's historical heritage should consider whether or not what they think they are saving is something living and authentic or simply a vague and mislead nostalgia for "the good old days." Are those in the trenches of the culture war fighting for something concrete or even intelligible to others? "I know you're set for fighting but what are you fighting for?[19]" Those on the "conservative" side of the culture war accuse the left or

---

[19] Song by Phil Ochs (1964). *What are you fighting for?*

"progressive" side of being driven by utopian ideas. This is however not limited to just the left, those on the conservative side tend to be equally utopian in what they expresses as their goals. One example includes defending Canadian national symbols and cultural heritage; the only problem being that much of the heritage of Canada has been relegated to museums, "heritage moments" trivia, and curiosity stores. Another example is the preservation of Canada's supposed Christian heritage; but Christianity just like any other religion lives through the daily practices of its followers, it is not something which can be imposed onto dead matter or unwilling participants but can only be practiced by a living spirit through community practice. Empty church pews are a telling sign.

The fundamental essence of what conservatives claim to be fighting for is the defense of history; the traditional telling of Canadian history is under fire for apparently not being compatible with progressive political sentiments held by contemporary "social justice warriors." "But a nation does not remain a nation only because it has roots in the past. Memory is never enough to guarantee that a nation can articulate itself in the present. There must be a thrust of intention into the future[20]." To say that the defense of Canada's history is what matters is to completely miss the point that Canada has long parted ways with that culture which is on display in Canadian

---

[20] Grant, G. (1970). *Lament for a Nation*. Toronto: McClelland and Stewart Limited in association with the Institute of Canadian Studies, Carleton University, pg. 12

iconography and ascetics. In fact the very cultural heritage that Canada was born out of blew itself up along with the rest of the Western world in the two World Wars of the first half of the 20th century; and even without those suicidal wars it is hard to imagine a world much different from the one we see today because of Western man's worship of "progress" and technological advancement whatever the consequences. After all, God had already been declared dead by the latter half of the 19th century[21]. Many of the values and sentiments that most conservatives see as their duty to defend have been sold off and replaced by new and shiny ones. It is ironic that those decrying the apparent attacks on Canada's way of life are not at all offended by the replacement of 19th sentiments with the commercializing, sexualizing, and dehumanizing ways of consumer culture. Even the commercial invasion and exploitation of Christmas seems incapable of stirring the passions of conservatives especially since there are more pressing matters to address like the use of "happy holidays" instead of "Merry Christmas." Perhaps Jesus was a capitalist after all, why else would he spend so much time hanging around the market place?

Canada's 2019 federal election will come and go just as all the others have. No matter the political rhetoric being used would have us believe is the case, the stakes could not be more mediocre and "normal" then they have

---

[21] The works by Friedrich Nietzsche do a wonderful job at expressing the impact on public thinking and its world view with the onset of the cult of science and worship of progress.

previously been. Liberalism is inherently a-historical so why should any party espouse of a shared destiny? Taken to its logical extreme liberalism *is* "post-national" so why should the state preserve specific heritages, cultures, or traditions? Canadians are simple and good hearted people who do not mind lending a hand, sparing a dime, at the same time they live materially comfortable (but of course like good consumers they are never fully content). Those parties who will do well in the next election are going to be those who grasp the sort of society Canada is; a society of tepid political passions concerned mostly with the daily commute and just getting by. To some it is a blessing to live in such a serene and sleepy society, but this is not without its costs.

The World

When compared with the political contests found in political arenas in the rest of the world Canada's political process is astonishingly tame and civil. Canadians take pride in their political system where it is the ballot that determines their representatives and where it is in the parliamentary debate that politicians make and shape the laws. Political violence is rarely seen in Canada and when it has crept up its extent has remained contained and quickly brought to an end using democratic laws. And why should Canadians *not* cherish and take advantage of their sleepy political arena? After all what political issues are left unsettled that cannot be dealt with through parliamentary debate or the legal system?

To most Canadians what we have managed to create is the inevitable product of the march of progress towards a more tolerant and peaceful world. The Canada of today can be described as what in the 1990's was a popular view of the world, "the end of history." Canada as a historical entity has reached the end of its political development, the end of its political history, in the form of a progressive liberal-democratic "post-national" state. It is hard to deny that Canada seems to have solved the political question by creating an environment where individual freedoms are married with a wide social welfare net resulting in a society that both promotes personal liberty and expression while ensuring a high minimum standard of living and a certain level of civil discourse; Canada has become the embodiment of the liberal ideal. Unfortunately for Canada however history has not in fact ended but has continued to march along despite what liberal internationalists may have wanted to see come out of the post-Cold War era.

If we take a look back at the decade following the end of the Cold War in 1989 and the collapse of the Soviet Union in 1991 we find a period of time where liberal idealists and internationalists rejoiced that out of the ashes of the 20th century mankind was finally going to achieve its dream of peace and stability on Earth. The future was free market liberal-democracy; our only trouble would be the fight against boredom.

The liberal character of Canadian society and politics is the product of Canada's own unique historical developments. By "unique" we mean not necessarily special or admirable but only that it is how the nation state of Canada has been shaped by its own historical developments and how it subsequently views itself and the outside world. These historical developments are based not only on the geopolitical realities of Canada but those of other powers also.

It is only natural that as the forces behind one world order recede that the forces previously held back will advance and take root wherever it is possible for them to do so. In preparing for the perceived "changing of the guard" it is natural for powers big and small to begin taking steps to pre-empt whatever may come their way[22].

This "acting with prudence" has shown its face in one particular way in the form of a new global arms race. With record military spending in America in order to develop and expand its military capabilities it was only a matter of time before other countries began following suite. Countries like Russia, China, Saudi Arabia, Iran, Japan, France, Germany, and the UK have been openly expressing their intentions to increase their military capabilities. In the case of Europe we have seen a trend develop towards the reforming and reorganizing of national armies into a single "European Army." It can only be assumed that what makes such an army "European" is going to be the interests for which it fights for; a European army would likely be independent of NATO and therefore of American interests.

The arms race did not come about suddenly as a result of the election of President Trump. It has been going on since the early years of the 21st century and has its roots in the last decade of the 20th century. Since the onset of American adventurism in the Afghanistan and Iraq other countries looking on watched as America put to work the previous generation's military equipment and technology.

---

[22] Niccolo Machiavelli illustrates the need to be prudent with his allusion to the changes of fortune, the tides of fortune being like a river occasionally swelling up and flooding its banks; in times of calm prudent men build up dams and levees not because it will prevent all flooding but because it will help manage the flooding. Machiavelli, N. (1992). *The Prince*. New York: Dover Publications, pgs. 66-68

The years following the collapse of the Soviet Union saw an assertive United States throw its military might all over the world and doing so completely unopposed by even the slightest use of military force, with the possible exception of China during the Taiwan Strait Crisis of 1995-96. What quickly became clear was that as the world passed further away from the immediate post-Cold War era those powers who wanted a piece of the action in the next century would have to rebuild their military capabilities. Russia stands as a prime example of a power that made the investments to stay in the game despite it not having the same super power capabilities the USSR previously had.

But there is one country that has begun to develop its military in a way that signals that it has no intention to simply be content with the American status quo but instead sees itself as the "logical" alternative to American power. China has not only modernized its army and power projecting capabilities but has begun looking outwards across the world for opportunities to plant the seeds of future military and geopolitical positions. In Africa we see China building its first "official" overseas military base in the East-African nation of Djibouti. In the South China Sea the world has watched as China began constructing artificial islands and then proceeded to build air bases on them. In Pakistan members of China's armed forces participate in war games alongside their Pakistani allies in a show of solidarity and willingness to deploy forces to face "external threats." In South America China has taken a huge interest in the continent's vast amount of natural resources along with its strategic geographical location in "America's backyard."

Although these developments have seemingly been modest and limited in their international implications it does however serve as a warning that other powers in the world are thinking that the possibility of great power war is not an impossibility and that it is better to be safe than sorry. The European Union has come to the realization that in a world of competing great powers it is likely to be in a position of weakness and may find itself in the middle of other great powers, particularly America and China, as they try to assert dominance over Europe. Just as in the Cold War Europe is quickly becoming an arena of competition for spheres of influence. If the EU wants to avoid being treated as an object to be acquired then it will have to deepen its integration process and foster a deeper feeling of belonging to Europe as a whole rather than as a confederation of nation states. The goal of an integrated European defense network will allow Europe to both defend its interests on the mainland and project power to enforce its interests abroad.

Canada is no exception to following the rule of maintaining preparedness for future conflict. Although Canada has not yet taken steps to build up its military capabilities it has been working towards reassuring its military partners of its continued commitment to the collective security agreements of NATO and NORAD. While these may be dismissed as relics of the Cold War they represent vital pillars to the world order that Canada has contributed to building. The preservation of NATO and NORAD are in Canada's interest if it wishes to continue to flourish as a liberal-democratic market economy; Canada's commitments are at the core of national and continental defense. So while the Canada of Prime Minister Trudeau has maintained a public image of being committed to peace keeping it is foolish to disregard Canada's security commitments to its allies and North America as a whole. If history has taught us anything it is that no matter how much we may want to avoid war it is uncanny how war tends to seek us out[23].

---

[23] "Let us not hear of generals who conquer without bloodshed. If a bloody slaughter is a horrible sight, then that is a ground for paying more respect to war, but not for making the sword we wear blunter and blunter by degrees from feelings of humanity, until someone steps in with one that is sharp and lops off the arm from our body." Clausewitz, C. (2004). *On War*. New York: Barnes & Noble, pg. 242

The Nation

The subtitle to George Grant's book *Lament for a Nation* is somewhat misleading at first glance. What does he mean when he says "The Defeat of Canadian Nationalism," and does Grant accurately identify those responsible for the defeat? The word "defeat" congers up images of some heroic battle where the forces of resistance are fighting all the way to the end. It would be a gross misrepresentation of historical facts to say that Canada was coerced and subjugated into accepting American commercial culture but then again it would not be honest if we claimed that Canada gave much resistance to the advancing Yankee way of life.

As with the rest of the Western world, Canada after the Second World War was dazzled by the glitz and glamour of the golden age of America's post-war boom. American music, movies, foods, consumer goods, and cars exploded onto the world market and captivated entire populations on every continent. The advertisement industry was kicked into overdrive to "inform" the consumer in every country of the free world why he or she *needs* the hot new gizmo and why the old one just won't cut it anymore; American culture displaced traditional and national cultures; American technological might shattered the antiquated ways of the past. After a decade of depression followed by the deadliest conflict in human history it was *finally* time for the common man to sit back and relax in the new world of comfort and ease. The only worry left to deal with was that pesky Soviet Union; those godless-commies would come around soon enough though and join the civilized world.

What has come of the Canada that existed at the time of Grant's writing? What did Grant actually think would become of the nation of Canada? What has come of Canada's sovereignty in light of American political, cultural, financial, and military domination? Canada remains in almost the same position as it did when Grant lamented over it in 1965. Canadians still regard themselves as "different from Americans" while embracing and emulating American popular culture. Canadians still celebrate and sing the praises of popular (and usually Democratic) American presidents and pay close attention to scandals in the realm of American politics and popular culture.

Canadians still prefer American music, television, movies, fast food, and popular culture over anything the CBC or local "Ma & Pa" shops can offer. Is this the fault of America or Canada? American power is undeniably immense both militarily and economically. As the world's preeminent military power and the world's leading economy it is understandable how Canada could be sucked into America's orbit especially given Canada's geopolitical circumstances. But there is an element of power which is easily overlooked because it does not fit into the images of "traditional" uses of power such as war and punishment. Power does not belong exclusively to the realm of physical force but is shared also by the realm of the mind. With all that can be accomplished through the force of arms, instilling terror and breaking willpower, the "sharing" of a common culture and the prosperity that follows its practice and fostering of good relations is just as potent in the exercise of power. Canada in a way has internalized Americanism while remaining non-American.

"Soft power," that which comes in the form of spreading culture, propagating ideology and political beliefs, and the extension of wealth sharing through economic cooperation, is a vital tool in the arsenal of all great powers. Soft power allows great powers to impose their will upon other states in a way that those states being subjected to the will of another finds difficult to resist because its effects are not obvious or are too lucrative and desirable to resist; resistance becomes a chore not worth the effort or price to pursue. A common practice in the use of soft power is the promoting of the greater power's culture and world view through a process of cultural exchange. The greater power shares certain aspects of its culture which carry with them the political essence of it. The American music and movie industries for example are deeply infused with "Americanism" and are vehicles which carry the nation's ideology. The goal of soft power is to foster positive feelings and sympathy in targeted populations towards the great power. Perhaps it is hard to believe that just because American movies and music are enjoyed in a country that this somehow means that

America has the power to determine that country's political and economic decisions. But what if over a period of decades of constant exposure to "American society" through various media a certain country begins to develop a sort of feeling of fraternity based on a desire to want to partake in the affluent and culturally rich society that America apparently has to offer? Is it really such a stretch to assume that a population in such circumstances would be more sympathetic to American causes in the world; after all if American society stands for such good things as their media portrays then it must be good that some Americans want to share their values with the world.

The cynic may consider the use of soft power as a form of manipulation pure and simple; the term "neo-imperialism" conjures up all sorts of images of exploitation of indigenous populations through the subversion of their local culture and the fostering of political corruption by means of the injection of foreign capital into a country. But it should be considered whether or not Canada is a victim of American soft power or if it is in fact a willing convert to a new way of life. The society on display in American soft power is one that is not alien to Canada despite what some may want to believe. Although a cultural staple of Canada used to be its honored place in the British Empire and then Commonwealth of Nations the idea of Canada being an extension of Britain and British power has fallen away as a relic of the pre-Second World War era when Britain and the other European powers were still in the preeminent position of world power. With the end of the European world order and the process of decolonization which followed it is both useless and ridiculous to hold onto the idea that Canada retains the position it once held as being Britain's representation in North America. The very opposite has become true in that Britain, the former eternal Empire on which the sun never sets, is now the unofficial representative of America in Europe. If this is the case then it would take a great feat of mental gymnastics to conclude that Canada is still too British to ever find American society even remotely tolerable. It must be accepted that Canada has been an active participant in the Americanization of its own society and by extension of its politics, economics, and foreign policy.

Every aspect of Canadian culture has been either Americanized or has been re-imagined into something that can be easily commercialized. Canadian television is mostly filled with American shows; promoting "Canadian content" is a sad attempt by government regulators to reverse or slow the process of Americanization by mandating Canadian elements into a field saturated with American content. Is Canadian culture noting more than beavers, maple syrup, *"Timmy's,"* and camping in a national park? Does dressing up a stuffed bear in RCMP uniforms really make it Canadian? One has to wonder over Grant's reaction to see his beloved "small town" Canadian culture being used to sell fast food, cheap clothes, and taxpayer funded cable television.

In short Grant was correct when he pointed to the Americanization of Canadian society as a major reason for Canada's cultural shift but perhaps he underestimated Canada's enthusiasm with the shift. Canadian nationalism was not so much "defeated" as it was put out to pasture when the realities of world affairs shifted. Canadians retained the window dressing of the independent nation state while becoming intertwined politically, economically, and culturally with America.

The Continent

The subtitle of this book is *Canada's Continental Destiny*. Destiny is something which is predetermined due to a combination of factors including elements inherent in design and subsequent historical developments. An undeniable historical development that has taken place since the middle of the 20th century, and despite Canada's historical resistance to the idea is the "continentalization" of politics, economics, and foreign policy. The global geopolitical competition that followed the Second World War was born from the global nature of the previous war.

The Cold War was a competition for control of the world order which was formerly controlled by the European Empires. After two suicidal wars Europe was economically, militarily, and morally exhausted and was therefore forced to relinquish control of the global order based on the imperial powers of Europe and turn it over to those countries powerful enough to fill the power vacuum. The end of the Second World War found two nations which because of their vast size and easy access to resources were left in a position to take advantage of the political vacuum left after the collapse of European prestige in the world. It appeared as though the prophecy of Alexis de Tocqueville had come true[24]; the United

---

[24] To quote de Tocqueville at length: "There are at the present time two great nations in the world, which started from different points, but seem to tend towards the same end. I allude to the

States of America and the Soviet Union were now the world's only great powers and each was determined to rebuild Europe and the greater world in its own image.

Over the course of the Cold War it became more obvious by the year that the competition being waged by America and Russia was changing how we traditionally looked at world politics. The nature of the Cold War was geopolitical in nature meaning that the actions of the great

---

Russians and the Americans. Both of them have grown up unnoticed; and whilst the attention of mankind was directed elsewhere, they have suddenly placed themselves in the front rank among the nations, and the world learned their existence and their greatness at almost the same time.

All other nations seem to have nearly reached their natural limits, and they have only to maintain their power; but these are still in the act of growth. All the others have stopped, or continue to advance with extreme difficulty; these alone are proceeding with ease and celerity along a path to which no limit can be perceived. The American struggles against the obstacles which nature opposes to him; the adversaries of the Russian are men. The former combats the wilderness and savage life; the latter, civilization with all its arms. The conquests of the American are therefore gained with the ploughshare; those of the Russian by the sword. The Anglo-American relies upon personal interest to accomplish his ends, and gives free scope to the unguided strength and common sense of the people; the Russian centers all the authority of society in a single arm. The principal instrument of the former is freedom; of the latter, servitude. Their starting-point is different, and their courses are not the same; yet each of them seems marked out by the will of Heaven to sway the destinies of half the globe." Tocqueville, A. (1998). *Democracy in America*. Ware, Hertfordshire: Wordsworth Editions Limited Cumberland House, pg. 170

powers were calculated to take into consideration how seemingly isolated interests and events related to the "big picture" of the global struggle. No longer was it possible to dismiss events on the other side of the globe, or "overseas," as unrelated to one's own nation's interests because every event in every part of the globe was *potentially* relevant to the balance of power. It was deemed prudent to see world events as "zero-sum," if one did not take advantage of a situation then one's enemy surely would. Either communism was advancing or democracy was; one could not sleep while the other was stirring. Freedom must be defended everywhere and the proletarian must be assisted everywhere.

The course of the Cold War revealed the existential challenge that continental defense posed. America as a single country within its own internationally recognized borders was a fundamentally insecure state in the new age of global thermonuclear war. The closing months of the Second World War signaled the beginning of the Nuclear Age and with it "intercontinental war."

As time marched so too did the development of more lethal and accurate methods of warfare. Battlefields of war had been liberated from the constraints of time and space to the extent that countries could now exploit technology which helped to minimize such limits that time and space once restricted; in the past a battlefield locked a nation's forces in a fixed position and moving such forces would require some amount of time. Rocket technology and the jet engine extended the reach of military arms and reduced the time which it previously took to deliver payloads. Nowhere on Earth was beyond the reach of these new weapons of war and this forced the "super powers" to consider their movements globally. If for example the armies of NATO and the USSR came to blows in central Europe this did not mean that in order for America to strike Moscow it had to fight its way and physically get within range, instead America was at liberty to strike Moscow by means of missiles launched from the United States. This was true for the Soviet Union also; if the USSR wished to strike the American mainland it didn't have to physically invade the continent but could instead launch a volley of ICBMs from Russia over the North Pole and towards their targets. Adding to the dilemma of the reach of payloads was the awesome destructive power available in the form of nuclear weapons. No longer could political and military leaders assume that clashes could remain "limited" because all potential flashpoints posed the risk of leading to nuclear war.

Man had finally achieved a level of technological development where he could, with the press of a button, strike his enemy anywhere almost instantly and at the same time bring about the destruction of the Earth itself. The nuclear arms race forced America and Russia to constantly match and attempt to surpass the other in scale, firepower, and reach of their respective nuclear arsenals. It was only natural that with the entire world at play in the game of global thermonuclear war there would follow a reaction to the ability to strike globally; what followed was the necessity to be able to defend globally. It is a part of the nature of war that new weapons and methods of fighting always inspire men to come up with ways of neutralizing those weapons and countering their enemies. Clubs and bladed weapons inspired shields, horses inspired long spears and pikes, rifles and artillery inspired trenches and dug-outs, tanks inspired tank-killers, and nuclear missiles inspired anti-missiles. The nuclear arms race was a race to develop the best weapons and the best defence against those weapons. Some "defensive" weapons came in the form of missiles designed to shoot down incoming enemy missiles. Coupled with missile systems were vast arrays of radar stations designed to detect incoming flying objects. Missile shields were considered by some to be a way to resist hostilities from the other side while others were more sceptical as to whether or not simply blocking or shooting down missiles would be enough to win the next war or even to survive it. What this doubt eventually gave rise to was the strategy known as deterrence.

Deterrence was thought by some to be the solution to the problem of nuclear war[25]; the core problem of nuclear war was that if the use of nuclear weapons was sanctioned in a clash between the super powers then it was not clear how the two sides could be brought back from a nuclear

---

[25] Brodie, B. (2007) *Strategy in the Missile Age*. Santa Monica, California: RAND Corporation, pgs. 271-273

exchange or what steps would necessarily follow a nuclear exchange. Theoretically each round of nuclear exchange would logically have to be met by another until one side finally surrendered and accepted defeat or until one side was no longer capable to responding due to its annihilation. But if it was possible to convince the other side before a nuclear exchange that one was capable and willing to finish the other side off in a single strike without the possibility of retaliation or launch a nuclear strike despite suffering great damage to one's nation then the enemy would be deterred from starting an exchange and thus one would not have to start one either. In other words the use of nuclear weapons in war had to be made potentially too costly for any power to even think about using and this would ideally cause powers to exercise self restraint.

Over the course of the Cold War there were numerous political and military theorists who explored possible scenarios of super power war and the concept of deterrence. Henry Kissinger, Bernard Brodie, Anatol Rapoport, Herman Khan, Erich Fromm, Kenneth Waltz, Samuel Huntington, and George Kennan are only a few of the theorists who discussed the concept of nuclear war and attempted to argue why or why not a given strategy would provoke or effectively render impotent the two super powers. Some argued that war as a tool of statecraft had become obsolete in the nuclear age and that the very presence of nuclear weapons made war impossible because of their excessive destructive potential[26]. Other theorists seemingly "learned to love the bomb" and attempted to convince their readers that in fact nuclear war should be considered as inevitable in great power competition; and since nuclear war is unavoidable then the nation's resources should be organized in order to prepare a strategy of pre-emption by unleashing one's entire arsenal at the earliest possible moment if circumstances so dictate and to organize society in such a way to "absorb" a nuclear attack at an "acceptable level" of destruction. Herman Khan, commonly regarded as the most "mad" of the nuclear theorists, forced his readers to "think the unthinkable" by accepting that nuclear war was both inevitable and possibly even survivable. Khan argued that since nuclear war was inevitable then the only way to defend against it was to convince the other side that no matter how much damage was sustained one could not only survive but retaliate and cause unacceptable damage to the other side. Even if America was hit by hundreds or thousands of nuclear weapons it would still have the potential of launching a retaliatory strike which would totally wreck Russian society. Some may find what he has to say as too dark and cynical for progressive and civilized peoples to even contemplate but then again it was these same progressive and civilized peoples and the leading scientific minds who invented the plague of nuclear weapons in the first place.

---

[26] See Anatol Rapoport's comments in the edition of Clausewitz's *On War*. Clausewitz, C. (1982). *On War*. London: Penguin Books, pgs. 11-80, 411-414

The onset of the Cold War and the nuclear era also revolutionized the concept of defence. The questions of what defense actually meant was now accompanied by the question of whose responsibility it was. With the entire world now in the line of nuclear fire defence became the concern of every country in the world. It seems that it was only natural that large political bodies would form in order to develop the concept of "collective security."

While military alliances are as old as history the form they took over the course of the Cold War was unique to the age. For instance there were two core competing camps who both consisted of a central leading state that enjoyed a large geographical core with abundant manpower and resources that it used to build up an organization of satellite states. America and Russia each formed the core of their respective military arrangements. Each core state had geopolitical influence over a number of friendly countries who served as extensions of the core country's power. The military arrangements headed by America took the form of NATO while those headed by Russia took the form of the Warsaw Pact. Each military alliance based itself on the promise to collectively defend each individual member while also coordinating military and security efforts towards a shared objective. The shared objective of NATO was the defense of the free world and democracy and the shared objective of the Warsaw Pact nations was the defense of Marxism-Leninism and socialism and championing the proletariat.

Aside from the arrangements made in NATO a separate arrangement was made by America and Canada specifically to address North America's geopolitical situation. This arrangement led to the formation of NORAD which aimed at securing the North American continent by coordinating Canadian and American military forces and infrastructure to create a security sphere around the continent. NORAD was essentially the Americanization of Canada's national defense into a larger continental defense.

The effects of the formation of NORAD were discussed by George Grant in his *Lament*. He saw the so called collaboration efforts between American and Canadian armed forces as an affront to Canadian sovereignty. If the basis for national sovereignty is a state's ability to defend itself then it is not unreasonable to believe that the absorption of Canada's armed forces into a larger grand design controlled by America will lead to a loss of Canadian decision making in matters relating to its sovereignty. If for example Canada was offered an opportunity to foster better relations with a state opposed to American influence in the world then the sitting Prime Minister of Canada would have to seriously worry about the American response to Canada's decisions and may even take action to block or dissuade Canada from taking a particular course.

The issue Grant took umbrage with the most was America's insistence that Canada, in order to enhance the security of North America, allow for the deployment of American nuclear weapons on Canadian soil[27]. He was most concerned with the social and political consequences of Canada becoming a quasi-nuclear armed power; Canada had prided itself as an authoritative voice for nuclear disarmament and arms control. It would be the height of hypocrisy for Canada to preach against the proliferation of nuclear weapons and lecture others about their uselessness while at the same time accepting nuclear weapons to defend its own soil[28]. This moral dilemma, whether or not Canada should accept American nuclear weapons on its soil, became known as the "Defense Crisis" and had very real consequences for Canada's domestic policies by helping to sink the re-election campaign of Prime Minister John Diefenbaker. Although America decided against insisting that nuclear weapons be deployed in Canada the damage was already done; Canada's national security was subject to American designs. Ultimately the "Americanization" of Canada's defense policies signaled the end of Canada's national sovereignty by effectively handing Canada's security resources over to America and its interests.

---

[27] See chapter 3 of Grant's Lament for a Nation Grant, G. (1970). *Lament for a Nation*. Toronto: McClelland and Stewart Limited in association with the Institute of Canadian Studies, Carleton University, pg. 25

[28] Of course most Canadians ignore the fact that Canada is nonetheless kept secure under America's "nuclear umbrella."

Whether or not Canada could have taken a different path by making different choices in its relationship with America is a contentious issue to discuss because of the ideological layers relating to developments in Canada and America. Canadians are fundamentally followers and supporters of American liberalism and the progressive view of history. Since the end of the Second World War Canadian society has continuously developed along the ideological lines set out by America especially those of the progressive school. Not only political but cultural trends in America are closely followed by Canadian society. America's advanced industrial society is admired by those Canadians who value consumer comforts and popular culture. The religious obsession of technology and the inherent "good" that comes from the passing of time is the unofficial state religion of Canada with New York City serving as Mecca and California serving as the Promised Land.

Political developments in America serve as a beacon to which Canadians dutifully turn their attention towards and endeavour to emulate. Even political trends that are popularly titled some sort of "mania" make their way into Canadian society. The "Trudeau-mania" that swept Canadian society in the late 1960's, and again beginning in 2015, were attempts to emulate trends in American politics. The first "Trudeau-mania" came shortly after America (and Canada) fell in love with President Kennedy, and the second onset of mania came after the election of President Obama. Just as America was over taken with "Camelot" and the Kennedy family so too was Canada head-over-heels for Jack; when the Obama family moved into the White House Canadians expressed a deep regret that he wasn't *their* president. But the love affair that Canadians have for certain American presidents is not some shallow political crush or intrigue like Canada has with British Royalty, Canada's infatuation with American leaders have policy implications. Canadians seem to "fall in love" with those American presidents who exemplify the ideals of liberalism and progressivism acceptable at the time. It is not a coincidence that the Democratic party enjoys more sympathy in Canada than the Republican party; the irony is that Canadians are seemingly oblivious that the two parties are ultimately two sides of the same coin and only differ in their rhetoric and views on how fast government power should be expanded.

What should be clear to anyone familiar with Canada-American relations is that while Canadian public opinion towards a sitting president may change from one administration to another this change from high to low favorability of the man in office always leads overall to closer relations. The hostilities towards one administration do not linger when its mandate comes to an end; the election of a new president grants forgiveness to whatever disagreement may have arisen. Following the course of Canada-America relations during the Cold War we see a continuation of the close relationship despite a few bumps along the way. The Vietnam war was just one such bump which was made especially bumpy with the election of

President Nixon. Up to the end of President Johnson's term in office Canada had patiently and quietly stood aside as America escalated its war in Vietnam. While not contributing soldiers or direct military support Canada did maintain its military sales to the American army throughout the war. When President Nixon took office in 1969 some noticeable policy changes were made by Canada which seemed to be more a jab at a president who was not particularly popular with progressive Canada. One example of a policy change was Canada's acceptance and protection of large numbers of military deserters and draft-dodgers. Another change was Canada's breaking with a number of issues in American foreign policy including officially recognizing the People's Republic of China. This was followed by increasingly warm relations between Cuba and Canada at a time when Cuba was assisting North Vietnam and trying to build closer relations with Russia. Although these policy changes on the part of Canada did not fundamentally undermine or threaten American security they did signal some political angst that Canada was feeling in its relationship with the United States.

Despite the rough patches between Canada and America, despite awkward interpersonal relationships between certain leaders of Canada and America the common path set forth since the end of the Second World War has not been abandoned by either country and is in fact becoming more inescapable as a joint endeavour. America knows that Canada will not set out on a course that would undermine American security in the Western hemisphere because Canadian security is deeply reliant on American power and its ability to maintain hegemony over the world order.

The end of the Cold War did not bring about the end of collective security; the security institutions constructed to defend against Soviet aggression continue to exist and have actually been expanded over the years following the end of the Cold War. Throughout the 1990's NATO remained intact as its continued relevance began to be questioned by politicians and policy makers of member nations. NATO was faced with an existential crisis brought on by the disappearance of an easily identifiable foe that served to justify its continued existence. The collapse of Yugoslavia and the religious and ethnic wars which followed served as an opportunity for NATO to reinvent itself as an upholder of human rights and Western values and even prove its worth as a potential policing force in Europe. It was argued that preserving NATO was necessary in order to maintain the peace achieved following "victory" in the Cold War and that disbanding NATO would only lead to chaos in Europe. But by the end of the decade NATO began going down a path which to some seemed at odds with its intended purpose. When NATO expanded Eastwards in 1999 by admitting Poland Hungary and the Czech Republic and laid out a frame work for further Eastward expansion it was becoming clear that American interests were going to be placed at the forefront in this new post-Cold War world.

Since the new era of NATO expansions[29], the latest being the admission of Montenegro in 2017, there has been a clear divergence in the interests of the major powers making up NATO. As the European Economic Community evolved into the European Union it began to signal that the interests of America were not necessarily shared by Europe and NATO began to show signs of having a split personality. The September 11, 2001 terrorist attacks against America saw for the first time NATO's Article 5, however reluctantly it appeared to be, implemented. The NATO coalition was activated to go after and destroy Al-Qaeda's terror network in Afghanistan. Once on the ground NATO forces were faced with the reality that the Taliban regime in Afghanistan was too dangerous to leave in power; if the Taliban allowed Al-Qaeda to build a network once then it was likely to allow Al-Qaeda or some other jihadist group to build up again. What was needed, the Americans argued, was to re-build Afghanistan into a democracy. As the "War on Terror" dragged on and mutated into a "nation building" mission it was clear that NATO needed to answer a serious question, would NATO become nothing more than an American tool of global power?

The 2003 Invasion of Iraq was another distinctive mark in the widening interest gap between Europe and America. When forming its "Coalition of the willing" America made appeals to its allies around the world to contribute to

---

[29] 1999, 2004, and 2009.

the military effort it was planning in order to "eliminate Iraq's weapons of mass destruction." The president of Iraq, Saddam Hussein, was said to be the modern embodiment of evil; his ultimate goal being to obtain nuclear weapons so he could launch an attack against America and its allies. Canada, along with a number of Western European states, did not join in that coalition. Prime Minister Jean Chretien, on March 17, 2003, announced that "If military action proceeds without a new resolution of the Security Council, Canada will not participate," which to some seemed to be a shining example of Canada "standing up" to America and asserting its national sovereignty. However, we find that behind the scenes Canada and America still as close as ever with Canada agreeing to increase its troop presence in Afghanistan just before the American led invasion of Iraq began. It was lost on the public that by contributing more support to the war effort in Afghanistan Canada was allowing America to free up resources and refocus them on Iraq.

Canada's public "refusal" to contribute resources to the American war effort in Iraq did not signal a shift in Canadian foreign policy from a pro-American stance to one independent of American interests. We need only consider how carefully Canada addressed the increasingly unpopular war in Iraq. When anti-war protests and demonstrations broke out around the world Canada too saw its fare share of demonstrations. But these demonstrations did not result in any substantive change in the Canada-America relationship. Those who praise Prime Minister Chretien's "refusal" participate in the Iraq war without UN authorization as a testament to Canada's love for peace or as a rejection of American "imperialism" are naïve at best and dishonest at worst.

Not only did Canada-America relations continue to thrive but just a few years later they would be marked by a new era of pro-American sentiment brought on by Canadian infatuation with America's next president. The election of President Obama in 2008 saw a wave of Kennedy-like fanaticism and admiration sweep across Canada. Canadian news papers, news shows, magazines, popular culture, and political discourse took on a markedly pro-Obama stance. Politicians on both the left and right quoted President Obama and tried to emulate his youthful energy and idealistic rhetoric. After eight years of putting up with the antics of "W." and Canadians having to play down their close relations with America they could now proudly declare their love for America and its leader. The unpopularity of the Iraq War took a back-seat and along with it the unpopularity of American drone strikes across the "Muslim world." As long as there was a progressive idealist, i.e. Democrat, in the Oval Office America was morally justified in all of its actions, at least in the eyes of Canadians.

Despite having a new and widely popular President in power, the growing disagreement among NATO members posed a huge threat to America's position in the world.

NATO had proved itself to be an effective deterrent of traditional enemies and a vital pillar of stability in Europe following the Second World War. On the basis of NATO membership the Western European members found the nucleus they needed to form the necessary institutions which would finally evolve into the European Union. Collective defense had been an inspiration for Europeans to push for closer relations and it served as an expression for the idea of Europe's shared destiny. A feeling of European fraternity began to grow and the future of European politics was looked towards with optimism; perhaps after centuries of "Brother Wars" Europeans would finally be able to build a society of shared interests and opportunities. In the post-Cold War world that feeling of shared destiny amongst European nations has resulted in a serious reconsideration of Europe's place in the world and how it as a single unit should relate to other countries and "blocks." The disunity that had plagued Europe with wars and which left it vulnerable to manipulation by outside powers had to be transcended.

While the decades following the Second World War and the subsequent rise of the American order has led to disagreement and tension between America and its European allies the same cannot be said about the relationship between Canada and America. While the end of the Cold War uncovered the growing number of fundamental disagreements between European and American societies, that same period brought Canada and America closer politically, economically, and culturally than ever before. NATO and NORAD remain at the center of Canada's security apparatus and there are no signs that this is going to change any time soon. The end of the Cold War and what was hoped to be the "end of history" brought about by the triumph of liberal-democracy was widely accepted amongst Canadians. The rise of neoliberal economics and hyper commercialization of culture that was embraced by the English-speaking nations in the 1980's was resisted against by Western Europe throughout the 1990's and into the 21st century. To many Europeans the "American way of doing business" was seen as an affront to the very character of European culture. The "Americanization" of Europe and how to resist it became a popular topic in European politics

Unlike her European allies Canada did not develop resentment towards American domination of the world order and the shifting of NATO's collective security intention into one of spreading and preserving American liberalism around the world. Europeans are faced with the challenge of preserving their unique cultural character at a time when the scars of the 20th century are still visible. In a world where Europe is no longer the central pillar of the global order and where two suicidal wars have caused lasting historical trauma in European society Canada, a former British colony and extension of its global empire, cannot fall back on a heritage or identity that no longer exists. While the European states saw the end of the Cold War as a chance of a renewal of European power and influence in the world Canada could not reasonably expect the British Commonwealth of Nations to suddenly take on a more significant role in the world. The "third way" ideology of human rights, corporate power, market economies, and social welfare were all bundled into the new crusade to reinvent the world in America's image. The spreading of American idealism and liberalism have since become Canada's *raison d'être* and Canadians have been more than willing to accept this and take up the fight.

Although American foreign policy pays lip service to humanitarianism as being its motivation for embarking on a policy of spreading liberal-democracy it is questionable whether or not it is sincere in its stated motivations. Canada on the other hand seems to be more genuine in its desire to act for humanitarian purposes despite not being to its benefit in the long run. Any zealot of an ideology, religion, or cause risks becoming so involved with the ideals of a movement that when disillusionment begins to develop an existential crisis occurs. A crisis of Identity is something that can turn one's life upside-down and cause one to make decisions detrimental to one's best interests. This does not mean that one should never support a cause but one should be cautious about how that cause develops and what happens when it begins to fall apart. In the years following the September 11, 2001 attacks and the commencement of the war in Iraq in 2003 American foreign policy has become more obviously based not solely on liberal ideals but on asserting its hegemony in the world order it played the central role in creating. And why shouldn't America desire to retain its position in the world? After all, American blood has been spilt around the world in order to bring about an age of unprecedented prosperity; and American prosperity has been reciprocal, those countries who sided with America during the Cold War were left in a much more developed and prosperous position in the 1990's than those who sided with the Soviet Union.

Pre-empting the charges of "imperialism" leveled against American foreign policy we should remind the reader that history must not be viewed via contemporary ideological prejudices and personal sentiments. Those Canadian idealists who decried America's invasion of Iraq in 2003 correctly identified the false narrative used to justify the war (that Iraq had or was developing weapons of mass destruction *including* nuclear weapons, and that it posed a threat to the entire world) but did not admit that the war and its consequences would favor North American interests no matter what the outcome was[30]. It is very common for those living in stable and prosperous societies to forget or ignore what goes into establishing *and* preserving the circumstances necessary for prosperity and stability.

---

[30] Consider that America was able to insert itself directly into a region of the world where hostile regimes formed during the Cold War; this was done at the expense of a regime that had since become hostile to America. By removing Iraq as a player in the Middle-East America was able to establish a base in the region in order to apply pressure to a number of "rivals": Iran, Russia, and Syria.

We have tried to lay out the reliance Canada has on the role America plays as the dominant power in the world order. We Canadians have long been reliant on American economic activity for the very existence of our economy. With the legacy of Canada's position of colony of Britain and therefore supporter of the motherland long discarded into historical memory Canada found economic salvation to the South at a time when America was taking up the mantle of super power and entering into an economic golden age. Since the early days of the Cold War, Canada's economy was been re-established into what George Grant termed a "branch-plant satellite[31]" of American economic power. It was only natural that economic relations extended into the realm of political and military relations. The global environment which has been so beneficial to American economic activity was and still is possible only because of continued military superiority and domination of global trade routes. If Canada is a stable and prosperous country then it is so because of its close relations with America and the position it enjoys safely tucked under the American security umbrella along with being geographically insulated from hostile foreign powers. So to those who decry American "imperialism" while at the same time singing the praises for Canada's support for international liberalism, its generous social welfare system, and positive economic trends it would be

---

[31] Grant, G. (1970). *Lament for a Nation*. Toronto: McClelland and Stewart Limited in association with the Institute of Canadian Studies, Carleton University, pg. 87

prudent to consider whether or not idealism and ideology is clouding your judgment because it is always easy to condemn others from a position of safety and comfort. From a position of comfort Canadian society has produced those who would even suggest a closer relationship with China at the expense of Canada's relationship with America; such an idea while being contradictory to Canada's liberal society is nonetheless attractive to those who smell potentially lucrative trade opportunities.

At a time when Europe was beginning to re-evaluate its military and security relations with America there has been no such similar process, at lease no serious one, taking place in Canada. Canada is more than happy to retain its close relations with America especially since it brings with it such economic benefits as business incentives and the outsourcing of major aspects and costs of Canadian security to a wealthier country. Despite the theorised economic opportunities a closer relationship with China promise Canada would be doing itself a disservice by supporting a society that is antithetical to Canada's traditionally liberal-democratic society. But a nation's wellbeing is not solely based on economic activity; national security transcends questions of trade. Canada remains staunchly committed to NATO and NORAD as they continue to serve as vital pillars of Canada's security and prosperity. It is arguable whether or not the same is true for Europe. Western European society since the Second World War witnessed an economic miracle that brought with it unprecedented wealth and social benefits. Western Europe enjoyed an economic boom which it applied to building an extensive social welfare system. Healthcare, schooling, infrastructure, and employment reform were what the peoples of Europe were given and eventually came to expect from their governments. There are those who are sceptical over Europe's "economic miracle" and claim that this prosperity was only possible because of the security umbrella that America extended over Western Europe both militarily *and* economically.

The rebuilding of Western Europe was subsidized and protected using American money and soldiers. In order to defend Western Europe from the march of the Red Army and to prevent a complete collapse of society which threatened to bring about the return of totalitarianism America saw fit to assist in the rebuilding of Europe. Once the Cold War ended the central reasons for America's intimate involvement in European security and economics evaporated. The decade of the 1990's was a paradoxical time in the relationship because of the strange circumstances brought about by the collapse of the Soviet Union. The Western half of Europe was the envy of the world because of its high living standards and liberal institutions while the Eastern half was attempting to rebuild society after decades of Soviet domination and arrested development under communism. It was apparent that for the time being America's continued interest in European security and economic matters was still warranted in order to assist the newly liberated half of the continent. Nearly two decades into the 21st century finds a strange situation in Europe where the Western half remains more or less independent of American aid, (aside from the military umbrella still extended over all of Europe and over important trade routes), while the Eastern part of the continent has become reliant on American aid and direct engagement in the form of overt military support. This is further reflected in the political attitudes which have developed in Europe: the Western states regard their continued arrangements with America as a hindrance to the full potential of the European Union while the Eastern states look to the United States as their close ally and friend in the defense against Russia and an increasingly centralizing European Union. Additionally, Western Europe has displayed a great amount of scepticism towards America's policies towards Russia since the outbreak of hostilities in 2014; the Eastern European countries have been more than happy to show their support for America if it means confronting their ancient enemy to the East.

The end of the Cold War was a time of great optimism for the next century. The ideology that emerged as the "victor" of the Cold War quickly took advantage of the optimism that embodies the *zeitgeist* and convinced many in North America that it was time to take advantage of the optimism and begin closer economic ties between the victors of the Cold War. Canadian society was completely overtaken by the euphoria felt by those who saw the end of the Cold War as a total vindication of the ideologies of liberal-democracy and free market economics. Now that the ideological struggle was over it was time to begin the globalization of liberalism. Never again would national borders and obstinate governments clinging to antiquated ideologies pose a serious obstacle to the spreading of liberal values.

In North America the drive to create a free trade agreement on the continent inspired many to begin considering international relations between Canada and America as a continental affair. With an American president who enjoyed general enthusiasm from Canadians, President Clinton's prestige not being tainted by scandal North of the border, the campaign to create a free trade agreement for the continent gained momentum and thus NAFTA was born. The free trade agreement included Canada, America, and Mexico in what was regarded as the future of international trade. Since the North American countries shared apparently similar geopolitical interests it was seen as logical that they should make their trading arrangements reflect the political realities of the day. Whatever one thinks of NAFTA it must at the very least be considered as prudent to begin planting the germs of an idea that would lead to an open discussion of "continental" matters. Just as the formation of NORAD forced Canadians and Americans to think like North Americans and begin considering how best to organize continental security NAFTA changed the focus of domestic economic matters to one that included continental trade systems. Politicians in Canada, Mexico, and America began to consider how the interests of one related to the interests of the others. Policy makers would now have to consider the impact that economic developments in one part of the continent would affect communities on the other side of the continent. Elected representatives would now have to worry about lobbyists from other NAFTA countries who could threaten to cause economic pain and discomfort to their constituents.

The situation on the North American continent at the beginning of 2019 is a testament to the geopolitical realities of the day. Despite what most Canadians would like to admit the election of President Donald Trump has not fundamentally altered Canada-America relations. Although Canadian politicians have played to their ideological base by "bashing Trump" and joining in the "(self-)righteous indignation" of those progressive minded people who detest Trump no politician, who finds himself or herself in a position to do so, has dared to take concrete steps that would alter in any way the relationship between the two countries. Moral condemnation does not alter military and economic arrangements.

Not only has the Canada-America relationship gone on but a fundamental aspect of it has been "updated" to reflect the increased intimacy of the relationship. President Trump had derided NAFTA as outdated and fundamentally "un-American," a danger to American industry, and just plain "stupid for America." He declared that if NAFTA was not "renegotiated" in favor of

American and continental interests then he would walk away from it completely. What followed after months of negotiations between delegates from the three countries of North America was a new agreement, the USMCA, which was said to be a "better deal" than NAFTA. Fundamentally the USMCA is the same set of arrangements as NAFTA but there is one major undeclared aspect of the new agreement and that is continental security. The new agreement seems to express great concern for the potential of non-North American states exploiting the former agreement in order to undermine continental security. NAFTA was said to be neglectful of the fact that there are forces in the world who seek to exploit weaknesses in North American politics and economic activity in order to undermine America's position as world hegemon. To some this idea is nothing more than a fantasy dreamed up by neo-conservatives and cold-warriors just looking for the next war to fight. But if one considers the geopolitical developments of the early 21st century then it is clear that not only has history not reached its end but is about to "return" with a vengeance. To be concerned with matters of continental security and geopolitical consequences is not to be dismissed as a "red scare."

One fundamental aspect of liberalism is the view of history that sees the march of time inherently bring good to societies and to the world at large. The passing of time means that old practices that are seen to "hold back" social developments and prevent the full blooming of individual potential are discarded as relics. Every year brings with it new inventions to make life more comfortable and enjoyable. Individual "fulfillment" is made more attainable to more people as new social and economic practices are introduced. Progress is worshipped as a demi-god; the march of time is its miracle. "Because it's the current year" is justification enough for introducing any policy deemed to be politically acceptable to the dominant ideology. In the "modern day" it is unthinkable that such things like international conflict let alone tension should exist. This view of history is briefly discussed by George Grant[32]. He explains that Canada's world view is fundamentally optimistic and its view of history is "progressive" in that it worships the current year and almost completely dismisses anything deemed "antiquated" as being a relic of the past. Developments in political and social matters must be embraced because to do so is to embrace "progress." One has to wonder if this aspect of liberalism is not further exasperated by the dominance of consumer culture where newness and trends are chased after on a weekly basis; which came first egoism or consumerism? To scoff at something, an idea or a cultural norm, simply because of its roots in an earlier time is the cult of progress taken to its extreme ends[33].

---

[32] See chapter 7 of George Grant's *Lament for a Nation*. Grant, G. (1970). *Lament for a Nation*. Toronto: McClelland and Stewart Limited in association with the Institute of Canadian Studies, Carleton University, pg. 88-90

[33] How can we escape the fact that the necessary end product of the religion progress is not hope, but a society of existentialists

Those who would protest the increasing integration of continental affairs would do well to first consider their own views on history. If like most Canadians they hold that "progress" in time is inherently good, that the simple changing of the calendar year necessarily entails social change, then it would be hypocritical to view continental integration as anything but good. Events around the world have developed in a direction where large continental blocs are increasingly taking on the role of the 19th century European Empires. The European Union, the Eurasian Economic Union, and the Belt and Road Initiative are only a few of the economic blocs/projects that have developed since the end of the Cold War. If some would have North America be the only region that does not follow historical developments such as continental integration or "closer cooperation" then let them at least admit that they are mistaken in their blind worship of "the now."

Whether or not it should be admired or pitied that Canadians live so securely that they can indulge in such fanciful and idealist views of the world is beside the point. What matters is that by the grace of geopolitics Canada is secure and will remain so as long as it helps to maintain the order which allows it to exist in comfort.

For those not directly involved in politics or military matters the rest of the world seems to be nothing more

---

who know themselves in their own self-consciousness, but know the world entirely as despair?" Grant, G. (1969). *Technology and Empire*. Toronto: House of Anansi Press Limited pg. 58

than a fantasy land where odd occurrences sometimes happen which require "security forces" or "peace keepers" to make things "right" again. This naïve and simple view of the world is too dangerous to be taken serious by politicians holding positions vital to Canada's relations with America.

The Alternative

"Your empire is now like a Tyranny: it may have been wrong to take it; it is certainly dangerous to let it go[34]." This quote attributed to Pericles by Thucydides in his *History of the Peloponnesian War* is one which likely sends chills down the spine of idealists and liberal zealots. The thought that one could actually defend something described as an "empire" let alone a "tyranny" is inconceivable to those progressive and liberal minded peoples whose only intentions are to spread liberal-democracy and upholding human rights. Thucydides' use of the term "tyranny" must be understood in the proper context. It is the continued bad habit of "contemporaries" to apply *their* views and understandings of words to past uses. "Tyranny" in its Antique sense was not what we in the early 21st century understand it to be. I brought up this quote in order to get the reader to reconsider his or her view of America's role as the sole super power and unofficial hegemon of the world order. To label America as a "tyranny" or to describe it as an empire is not unfounded as long as one keeps things in perspective. The liberal rules based world order requires an unflinching willingness to enforce those customs and norms which have come to be regarded as acceptable practice by nation states. If the liberal world order created after the end of the

---

[34] Thucydides, (1972). *History of the Peloponnesian War*. London: Penguin Books, pg. 161

Second World War is to continue functioning then it will be necessary for those powers in a position to do so to preserve and enforce the order by whatever means necessary. To expect any order to go on functioning without any thought of enforcement or maintenance is not reasonable. If America stands as the head of the current order then it would be suicidal for it to allow the order to decay into something harmful to its own interests; the loss of financial power for example would directly lead to a loss of much needed capital for military expenditure.

The fact that American interests are expressed through liberalism is reason enough for America to remain at the forefront of its cause. If it is "tyrannical" for America to use its military and economic might to uphold a liberal rules based world order then let us remember a quote from Prime Minister Pierre Trudeau: "there are a lot of bleeding hearts around who just don't like to see people with helmets and guns. All I can say is, go on and bleed, but it is more important to keep law and order in this society than to be worried about weak-kneed people who don't like the looks of a soldier's helmet.[35]" To bask in the comforts of a way of life while shrinking from doing what is necessary to preserve it is the height of hypocrisy and a recipe for disaster.

Let us consider what could happen if Canada suddenly came to its senses and asserted its national sovereignty,

---

[35] Spoken during an interview with Canadian media, including the CBC, on October 13, 1970.

American interests be damned. Canada is going-it alone in its crusade for liberalism. Yes Canada will remain liberal whatever condition its relationship with America is presently in. Canada was born out of a British Empire that prided itself as being the embodiment of 19th century liberalism. It can be assumed that the liberal foundations of Canada are strong enough to weather the storms of time and remain fundamentally intact.

If we assume that Canada's liberal character would remain unchanged despite the state of its relationship with America then why is Canada seemingly so reluctant in chart a different path from America? It must be asked what sort of "different path" Canada could actually take and how that path would differ from the one it is on now. Before we begin to think of Canada's "options" we must first consider where Canada stands today. Presently Canada is a North American country with a landmass of nearly ten million square kilometers and a population of approximately thirty-seven million people as of 2019. It has a GDP of nearly two trillion dollars and America is its largest trading partner. Canada is a member of NATO, NORAD, the G7 and G20, and the United Nations, just to name a few. As a middle-power Canada has historically been an advocate for the global rules based order which holds at its core the United Nations declaration of human rights. In short Canada is a wealthy, industrialized, and stable nation state based on 19th century British liberalism.

We have briefly considered where Canadian society thinks it stands today but next we must consider where exactly it stands as a "global player." As a member of the United Nations Canada recognizes the legitimacy of international law based on the order established after the Second World War. This order advocates for restraint to be exercised in international relations in instances of hostilities or disagreements. The UN stands at the centre of the order as the institute responsible for promoting mediation between belligerents and the easing of tensions in the world though the promotion of political accountability and human rights. Canada is a vocal advocate of the role the UN seeks to play as a pillar of international law. Canada has become associated with the UN's peacekeeping program and has participated in a number of peacekeeping missions around the world. In short Canada has ideologically aligned its foreign policy with the spirit of the international order promoted by the UN and rooted in liberal internationalism.

If Canada is to be viewed alone inside a global political vacuum then we find a nation state who takes the idea of "global citizenship" as its *raison d'être*. But Canada does not exist in a vacuum and geopolitics has a real impact on Canada's idealist policies just as it does on the policies of every other country. Canada for example is slightly larger than the United Sates and has access to vast natural resources but at the same time it has a population one tenth the size of the US. Geographically the terrain of Canada is less hospitable to large human populations while a great part of its land, while stunningly beautiful, is not conducive to developing large industries apart from farming, mining, and oil extraction. Canada's history differs from that of America's in that it remained an important part of the British Empire for much longer than the rebellious United States and even after Canada's official founding as a country in 1867 it remained closely linked with British imperial policy. When the British Empire disappeared following the Second World War Canada was left holding onto a heritage whose roots had been fundamentally severed from its motherland while at the same time leaving Canada in a semi-colonial mind set. The United States on the other hand had declared its independence from the British in 1776 and since then had built its society into an industrialized yet self-sufficient state with huge military potential which was finally unleashed in 1917 and later on in 1941 resulting in America taking effective control of the world order established by the former British Empire.

If one remembers that Canada considers itself a liberal-democratic society based on the ideology of liberalism then it is understandable why the world seems to it so simple to Canadians. Idealism allows the thinker to remain in the realm of the unreal where thought is not constrained by hard realities. Those Canadian idealists who would have Canada simply break off relations with America base these arguments not on the dictates of reality but on ideologically tinged "logic." Overzealous belief in liberal internationalism sometimes causes Canadians and even

Americans to decry the role the United States plays in the world; the title "world police" is a mixture of the recognition of America's pre-eminence and a denouncement of American imperialism. Even President Trump successfully wielded public exhaustion in American military adventurism; while simultaneously building American military power projection Trump promises that America will no longer be the "police of the world."

Since the end of the Cold War the trends in international relations have not gone in the direction that liberal internationalists thought it would. From a world order based on a system of "bi-polarity" between American and Soviet power the post-Cold War world is increasingly showing signs of a system based on "multi-polarity." The rhetoric of liberalism has remained intact but its practice in real institutions or political trends have not remained unchallenged. Where has Canada's espousal of liberal internationalism left it two decades into the 21st century? What has become of Canada the "nice" country in a world increasingly going down a different path than was predicted it would go by the Hegelians and Marxists, or as George Grant thought it might[36] but instead the path outlined by Samuel Huntington in his *Clash of Civilizations*. Huntington correctly identified that the

---

[36] See Chapter 5 of George Grant's *Lament for a Nation*. Grant, G. (1970). *Lament for a Nation*. Toronto: McClelland and Stewart Limited in association with the Institute of Canadian Studies, Carleton University, pgs. 53-67

future trend of international relations would be strongly influenced by historical identity based on notions of civilizations and the world views they form. By the middle of the 20th century it was clear that the world order created by the European great powers over the course of centuries was effectively dead. But the death of the European order was deferred because of the onset of the Cold War between the world's two super powers. The rise of the super powers meant that political and military concerns for most of the world would be overshadowed by the bi-polar power struggle between America and Russia. The collapse of European power and prestige in the world was logically followed by a wave of national liberation movements across Asia and Africa but their perceived intention of national self-determination and indigenous political interests was quickly commandeered by the ideological struggle of the Cold War. What resulted were numerous wars of national liberation which saw political factions making appeals to one of the two super powers to lend assistance at the cost of ideological loyalty. This was the nature of nearly all wars which followed the end of the Second World War right up to 1991 when the Soviet Union finally collapsed. Huntington was one of the theorists who correctly saw the end of the Cold War not as a ceasing of hostilities but as a great releasing of passions and hatreds which were previously suppressed by the bi-polar world.

Despite international developments showing signs that the old order is collapsing Canada still remains one of the most vocal advocates for preserving and strengthening the international institutions created following the Second World War. Its insistence that international relations be conducted based on the rules based world order has given it a sense of self admiration for being a staunch defender of liberalism and human rights. But once again Canada is being confronted with an existential crisis brought on by the march of history and the reluctance by Canadians to see the world as it actually is rather then as it ideologically should be. In 1945 Canada was left in a politically confusing situation and was forced to realign its self image to reflect the realities of the day. When the British Empire had finally exhausted its political power as the director of world affairs and subsequently handed the torch to the United States Canada essentially followed the new holder of world power. The enthusiasm with which Canada went along with American idealism was of the nature of a colony standing by its imperial motherland. The developments of the Cold War and how to address them became natural to Canada as it took up the new crusade of the United Nations and the "free world" as defined by the United States. When the Cold War came screeching to a halt Canada was once again left holding onto a currency that seemingly had lost its value.

Since the end of the Cold War the world has seen the rise of a number of regional bodies which have become more sovereign in nature as time goes by. Talk of regional integration once dismissed as foolish or even dangerous is now taken very seriously as a "solution" to the problems of conflict and poverty[37]. Huntington's insistence that as the political influence of Europe is expelled from most regions of the world there would follow a renaissance in historical indigenous identities based on patters of civilization has seemingly come true in the implementation of various economic unions defined along the lines of shared racial, cultural, and religious grounds. The pooling of resources to promote regional and cultural interests in matters of economics, politics, and security concerns goes against the popular views of the post-Cold War world which saw a future where internationalism results in a stronger international system based on liberal-democracy of the American strain accompanied by free trade and an international free market. The suggestion that cultural identity or religious affiliation could play *any* role in the future of international relations was regarded as backwards in its thinking and even racist in its logic.

In a world reorganizing itself along the lines of civilizational, cultural, and historical identities where does Canada fit in? The logical home for Canada in a world of regions is none other than North America. But for those who would insist that Canada resists the urge (and defy reality itself) of regionalism the alternative options are in fact very limited and even dangerous. If Canada was to step out of the American world order then it would be quickly faced with a world of states who are cunning,

---

[37] Huntington, S. (2002). *The Clash of Civilizations*. London: Free Press, pgs. 21-29

deceitful, self interested, and jealous of Canada's land and resources; in other words international relations as usual.

Where has Canada's insistence on an international rules based order and international institutions gotten it? In 2014 when hostilities between Russia and Ukraine came to a head and Russia asserted its self identified sphere of influence in Eastern Europe the world (the Western world to be exact) was outraged. Not since the Gulf War had there been a nation flaunting its complete disregard of international borders and sovereignty by interfering in the "internal" politics of its neighbour. The condemnation of Russia's intervention in Eastern Ukraine and the organizing of an independence referendum in Crimea, resulting in it joining the Russian Federation, was led by an outraged President Barack Obama who insisted that such actions on the part of Russia were from the 19th century and did not belong in the modern day. Canada enthusiastically joined alongside the European Union in echoing America's condemnation of "Russian aggression." As a consequence for its actions Russia was sanctioned and expelled from the G8 which was then rechristened the G7. Prime Minister Harper was applauded for his brave confrontation with President Vladimir Putin of Russia. "Get out of Ukraine" were the words used by Prime Minister Harper as though such a public chastisement was *really* going to do anything other than make a good anecdote. But actual results did not matter as long as Canada remained loyal to its belief in the rules based order.

The leadership of America and its role in enforcing the liberal order against a "revisionist" Russia helped reinforce Canada's belief that finger waving and lecturing could achieve anything tangible. The declaration by President Obama, that due to its own actions "Russia is isolated in the world," was what Canadians desperately wanted to believe. But it was not long before some countries made moves to prove to the world that in reality it is power and economic necessity that matters and not lofty ideals and sentimentality; after all a country has to eat and economies have to grow.

Within a span of five years since the events of 2014 a distinct dividing line has formed in Europe reflecting two different attitudes towards Russia. In the Eastern part of the continent, those countries that were once part of the Russian Empire and then Soviet Union or were one of its many satellites, remain staunchly in favor of confronting Russia for flaunting international law. Also in this camp are two traditional opponents to Russia namely Great Britain and America. Canada is in this camp too and remains shoulder to shoulder with those who see a "revisionist" Russia as the greatest, and seemingly the *only*, threat to the world order. On the other side of the dividing line are the countries of Western Europe who have increasingly been signaling to Russia and to the world that the European Union has a "different" set of interests, ones which are distinctly "European." While originally joining in with the condemnation of Russian actions in Ukraine countries such as Germany, Belgium,

France, and Italy have since signalled a desire to let bygones be bygones and move forward with building economic relations. The Western European countries view the conflict between Ukraine and Russia as one which was caused by both sides acting in bad faith; Ukraine is not a victim of aggression but an instigator of conflict.

That the countries of Western Europe should be less enthusiastic than those of the East in following along with American led condemnation campaigns and threats of military action is a reflection of historical developments that has the European Union increasingly parting ways from with "American interests."

What is Canada to do in a world where countries can choose not to follow liberal norms? Despite Canada's best efforts Russia has succeeded in preventing Ukraine from becoming a member of NATO and Russia has successfully asserted its interests in the Black Sea; the retaking of Crimea and overtly assisting the breakaway provinces in Ukraine's Donbass region are just a few examples of Russia asserting its national interest at the expense of the interests of Canada and America. The sanctions, verbal condemnation of Russia, and military and financial aid to the government in Kiev have left Canada little to show for its efforts besides lofty rhetoric and cheap propaganda. Not only has Russia been successful in asserting its interests in that part of Eastern Europe but it has also been successful asserting them elsewhere including in the Middle-East and the Arctic region. As the country with the largest Arctic coast Russia is not unreasonable when it asserts its place as a key player in the Arctic. As climate change and developing technology make the Arctic a more active geopolitical arena Canada, as an Arctic power, will have to come to terms with the potentiality that its sovereignty over its Arctic territory may be directly challenged by Russia and other powers. Unfortunately for Canada confronting and resisting a nuclear armed military giant is neither easy nor cheap. Any future moves to prevent Russia from impeding on Canadian territorial claims in the Arctic will have to be done so with the assistance of Canada's close ally the United States. The Arctic region is a prime example of the need to think continentally about security.

It is important to keep in mind that these developments are the result of a joint effort by Canada, America, the United Kingdom, and other allies. It is extremely unlikely that Canada would have been able to achieve any alternative outcome if it adopted separate policies towards addressing such an event as the Russia-Ukraine conflict. The same goes for Canadian foreign policy in general, it fundamentally requires allies both military and moral support.

The Inevitable

The quote at the beginning of this book likely causes the faint of heart much distress; to think that the "good" and "moral" and "decent" country of Canada, along with its shining culture, could be swallowed up by the great imperial power that is America is unconscionable; and to think that it would do so as a willing participant in the process is offensive. Should a "small" power be allowed to be offered up on the altar of the strong simply by virtue of a discrepancy of military and economic power? The difference in the power enjoyed by Canada and America is not something immediately comprehensible by the Canadian masses. To most Canadians the idea that America somehow has power *over* Canada is both offensive and unbelievable. Although it is widely accepted in Canada that America is the world's most powerful country what it actually means to have such power is lost on those who have not given the question a thorough exploration.

The very nature of Canadian society dictates that it will always take a path similar to those other liberal-democracies that share similar political cultures. That Canada would eventually be absorbed into America's sphere of influence should not have come as a surprise to any clear sighted and realistic observer. It is in the nature of power that those in its proximity are going to be subject to its force unless it has the power to resist the other's influence; a country that finds itself in such a situation has to face the choices dictated to it by reality, either submit or risk extinction.

For those who subscribe to the liberal school of thought the suggestion that an entity has the right to dictate its will because it has the power to do so is a violation of one of the sacred tenants of liberalism, inherent rights of self-determination. The ideological nature behind the use of the term "rights" blinds its users to the unkind reality that such rights are only worth as much as their enforcement carries them. Canada is a sovereign nation state and a member of the international community of nations and therefore has certain rights as a country. This is not disputed by liberals, what I am trying to make clear is that the rights Canada has as a country, self determination, the making of its own laws, and carrying on economic activity and enjoying the fruits of its labour are subject to existing forces beyond its control and outside its borders. These forces include geography, economics, and above all else the interests of other powers especially America. The right to self-determination that *any* country has is always subjected to the scrutiny and will of those countries that have the power to either promote or deny such rights[38]. This is the nature of things

---

[38] See John Mearsheimer's *The Tragedy of Great Power Politics* for an insightful discussion on the nature of anarchic nature of international relations. Mearsheimer, J. (2003). *The Tragedy of Great Power Politics*. New York : W. W. Norton & Company, pgs. 29-54

that is inherent in the international order and in human societies in general. The international "state of nature" dictates that power makes the law by enforcing the law. Law enforcement presupposes the means to do so.

It is not reasonable to simply declare something to be self evidently "the right thing to do" and expect it to be done in that way based solely on moral grounds. Perhaps the one who said it best was Machiavelli: "the manner in which we live, and that in which we ought to live are things so wide asunder, that he who quits the one to betake himself to the other is more likely to destroy himself than to save himself.[39]" Canada is one such country who would like to think of itself as a role model of liberalism in action. But is it reasonable to expect that in a world such as our own, one which is so rich in cultural diversity and subsequent word views and where unique historical experiences are an important defining factor in shaping the individual national characters of the world's countries, that advocating for a single political system inspired by a particular ideology is going to actually result in the spreading of liberalism without the use of force or coercion? And if force or coercion is required to promote liberalism then is this not a violation of a fundamental part of the ideology, self-determination.

The ideology which Canada holds dear to its heart, liberalism, represents an existential challenge to Canada as

[39] Machiavelli, N. (1992). *The Prince*. New York: Dover Publications, p. 40

a nation state. In a post-national era how can one justify defending the existence of Canada as a sovereign state when the dominant trend seems to be a movement towards regional union and internationalism? The European Union is a case in point. The year 2019 is a pivotal year in Europe's post-Cold War history. In May Europeans across the continent will cast their vote in the European Union parliamentarian elections[40]. This particular election is important in gauging the political trends throughout the EU. Since its last parliamentary election in 2015 Europe has seen the rise of populist, nationalist, and anti-EU/Euro-sceptic movements on the national level. These movements have already caused great political upheavals across the continent. In 2016 the elites of Europe were horrified as they watched a majority of British people vote in favor of leaving the EU. In France the presidential elections of 2017 saw the complete collapse of the country's traditional parties and the surge in support for nationalism at the same time an establishment technocrat was elected as president[41]. That same year saw the general

---

[40] At the time of this writing the European parliamentary elections resulted in many nationalist MPPs winning seats. The traditional ruling blocs, the liberals and socialists, both saw a poor turnout and must now attempt to reconcile with the new shape of European politics if the European Union is to have any hope for remaining intact and true to its founding principles.

[41] Since November of 2018 France has been rocked by demonstrations. Across the country demonstrators calling themselves the "gilets jaunes" or "yellow vests" have been demonstrating every weekend calling for the resignation of President Emmanuel Macron.

elections in Germany result in a nationalist party making gains previously thought to be impossible in a post-WWII Germany while the establishment parties had their worst results since the end of the Second World War. In Italy the political order established in that country following the end of the Cold War was wiped out and replaced with a coalition government of left and right wing parties who share a common nationalist platform and demand reform in the EU[42]. Then there were a number of standoffs between Brussels and various Eastern European countries who outright reject trends in the EU which to them signal that the EU is leading towards a closer federal union. A number of Eastern European states, Poland and Hungary in particular, have since reaffirmed their rights to make their own laws without regards to EU guide lines.

In all the above mentioned cases there is a distinct division between what is regarded as politically acceptable and what is not. By politically acceptable we mean that it adheres to international liberalism of the kind popularized

[42] Since this initial writing the government of Italy has gone through a change in political alliances. In Italy's European Parliamentary Election in May of 2019 the right-wing Lega Party became the largest political party representing Italy in Brussels. By August of 2019 the political coalition of the Five-Star and Lega Party broke down and a general election seemed imminent. But elections were avoided by the formation of a new political alliance between two former enemies, the Five-Star and Democratic parties. With the forming of a new coalition government Italy's populist and Euro-sceptic momentum has been temporarily arrested.

in the 1990's. Those deemed to be in contravention of ideologically acceptable policies are labeled racists, Nazis, nationalists, extremists, anti-liberals, "far-left/far-right," and populists. The only ideology acceptable to those in positions of power is one which has the European Union developing into a liberal super state that is economically and militarily sovereign and who defends globalization. A rhetorical line in the sand has been drawn with one side in favor of the "European project" and the other side calling for disintegration and chaos. The political rhetoric that is currently in fashion labels all those who support the EU as inherently "good" and those who oppose it as inherently "bad." This political rhetoric has caused such confusion in public discourse and has resulted in political debate devolving into episodes of hysteria over the rise of "right-wing extremism."

Whatever might be said about the results of the British referendum of 2016 it should be noted that the Britain seemingly voted along traditional political lines with regards to its relationship with continental Europe. "Brexit" is said by some to represent a desire for British sovereignty. This makes sense when we look back over Britain's historical relations with the various continental powers. While generally being regarded as a European country, Britain has usually stood aloof from the continent; Britain has always charted a different set of policies when it comes to European politics. One needs only consider the centuries of history which saw Britain do everything possible not to be subjugated by the dominant power in Europe, be it Spain, Austria, France, or Germany. Alternatively British policies towards Europe have always been motivated by the British preference of not allowing any single European power to dominate the continent; making an alliance with weaker states in order to oppose a rising state was common practice in British foreign policy. British interests have been shaped by its inherently international world view which itself is shaped by the geopolitical uniqueness of Britain. As an island off the coast of the European continent British territorial security is granted a boost by the forces of nature and can therefore instead turn its attention and resources to the Atlantic Ocean, its gateway to the world. However, "Brexit" represents not a return of British sovereignty as a world power but as an important member of Atlantic defense and subsequently North American defense. Without publically admitting to it Britain has declared to the world that it is a part of America's security apparatus rather than Europe's and as the EU becomes a more integrated entity with independent military capabilities America will come to rely on Britain as an extension of American power into Europe.

The outcome of the 2019 European elections will be a signal to those on both sides of the ideological divide in Europe. If there is a pro-EU outcome then the leaders of Europe will claim vindication and press on with current trends of gradual integration. If anti-EU forces make significant gains then this rebuff of the establishment will force the leaders of the EU to double their efforts to integrate the nations and achieve EU sovereignty over the nation states. If the latter outcome manifests itself then we can be sure that those who have spent the last few decades working towards the "European project" will not quietly accept defeat but will instead work harder and with more urgency to convince the peoples of Europe to finally overcome their regional prejudices and think continentally.

For those who attempt to defend the *status quo* in the European Union the most potent weapon in their rhetorical arsenal is to label their opponents as bigots. Whether the labeling of opponents of the EU as bigoted is fair or not is politically irrelevant because of the effectiveness of the tactic of smearing one's opponent with odious labels. A large portion of the debate over the future of the EU is nothing more than propaganda; either Europe will unite and usher in a new golden age or it will disintegrate and end up in a new world war. And to be fair the use of propaganda is not limited to one side or the other. Elements of the Euro-sceptic camp are guilty of using hyperbolic propaganda to convince people that there is a conspiracy to replace ethnic Europeans with non-Europeans or that "Judeo-Freemasonry" is attempting to eradicate European culture and replace it with "cultural-Marxist" ideology; to some Euro-sceptics the EU is the end result of a conspiracy aimed at destroying Europe. While these sorts of claims are derided and ridiculed in the media as examples of extremism in the Euro-sceptic camp the same "extremist" label is mysteriously not applied to those in the pro-Euro camp who spread equally hyperbolic propaganda. Elements in the pro-Euro camp have been more than happy to spread claims that gangs of Nazis and extremists are on the march or that any attempt to resist EU integration by a member state is an attempt to destroy the EU and democracy or that foreign powers are using Euro-sceptics in order to undermine European sovereignty. In order to further delegitimize populist and nationalist movements claims are even made that Russia or America are behind the movements in Europe. While such use of propaganda may seem below the dignity of liberal-democratic societies who pride themselves as being arbiters of "truth" and political morality it must be remembered that liberalism is nothing more than a political ideology and like all other political ideologies it is concerned with gaining and retaining power.

Canada's relations with the European Union reflect the deep roots of liberal ideology driving Canadian policies. Canada is a staunch supporter of the EU because of the trade opportunities that a more integrated EU promises, but it also sees the EU as the fulfilment of liberalism on the continent. Ideologically speaking, the European Union stands as the fulfilment of the promise made in 1945 that Europeans should never again allow differences of race, religion, culture, or nationality to drive the continent to another war. Following the Second World War nationalism was "thrown onto the ash heap of history" never to be allowed to possess the souls of Europeans again. From then on out Europeans would work through their differences diplomatically in order to bring the continent closer together and safeguarding the continent from stumbling into another war. Following the end of the Cold War the idea that there was a common European destiny had gained momentum in the idea of a future political union of European states. The EU presents its existence as everything that liberalism has to offer: the rule of law promotes "social justice," the "dignity of the individual" takes precedent over the claims of "the group," the primacy of "individual identity" is regarded as the standard by which social norms are to be measured by, traditional institutions such as religion, cultural practices, and social norms are subjected to the march of "progress," social welfare institutions and social safety nets are expanded to their furthest extent as a matter of obligation the state has in honoring the social contract, and above all markets and banking hubs are worshipped as "civilizing" forces in human society. To many Canadians and even left-wing Americans the idea of the European Union has taken the role in political rhetoric previously occupied by the promised utopias of the past.

If the European Union has come to represent the liberal ideal and if it is to be held up as an example to the rest of the world that ancient prejudices and hatreds can be overcome then it only makes sense that similar developments should take place around the world. Canada's close relationship with America has developed along a path of ever closer collaboration in matters of security, economics, and defending liberal values; why should the relationship arbitrarily stop before it culminates in some sort of political union? Are the differences between Canada and America so fundamental to their beings that they cannot be overcome for the greater good of continentalism? Since the election of President Trump one would be hard pressed to find many people who wouldn't dismiss the idea of a North American Union straightaway as something unthinkable. It is understandable why so many Canadians disapprove of President Trump; Trump represents an American movement which has revolted against the liberal establishment while most Canadians have not come to the point of even questioning the establishment let alone challenging it. It is not my intention to condemn or defend President Trump, all I will say is that ideology has much to do with how one sees the world[43]. Besides, the public always loves to hate a "bad guy."

What must be taken into consideration is that despite certain presidents being unpopular with the Canadian public the relationship between Canada and America has remained unscathed and has continued to grow stronger. For example in 2018 Canada's Prime Minister Trudeau signed Canada onto a new continental free trade agreement, the United States Mexico Canada Agreement, which is supposed to replace NAFTA and bring

---

[43] There is a quote from Dr. Henry Kissinger which is quite illuminating when it comes to understanding the varying interpretations of events: "the media can tell one what is happening but not what it actually means."

continental trading into the future. An important difference that the USMCA represents compared to NAFTA is the distinctly "continental" character that the new agreement emphasises in the realms of labour and technology, economic activity, and security. While NAFTA was essentially an unrestricted free trade agreement between Canada, America, and Mexico the USMCA takes very seriously potential threats to continental security that trade with non-North American countries may pose. It is difficult to predict what the consequences of this new agreement may be for the future of North American politics but if the evolution of the European Union serves as an example, going from a loose trading block to a common market to a political union, then it is not unrealistic to assume that in the foreseeable future some entity along the lines of a "North American Union" would be formed especially if the geopolitical competition between America and China ramps up.

I have tried to make clear to the reader that despite Canada's best of intentions while serving as a staunch advocate for liberalism overarching geopolitical realities will ultimately have the final say in international relations.

International trends in the last decade have been signaling that the United States world order is increasingly coming under scrutiny by powers that see it as a hindrance to their own interests. The developments in European politics have signaled a desire to build up the European Union into a power that can resist having to go along with

American plans that do not represent the interests of Europe. The rise of China is another international development that has come to represent the most serious challenge to American interests in the world and by extension the liberal world order.

By far the biggest geopolitical concern facing Canada has to be the developing competition between America and China for control over world markets. Canada is once again on the front line in the fight to preserve the American world order against forces that seek to undermine American pre-eminence. For all the good in the world that Canadians think they have done in promoting international norms and the rules based system, it has been like being dunked into a bath of cold water to learn that in the big picture all that matters is power and the ability to enforce one's interests. As we have already said above the end of the Cold War signaled to idealist liberals that now was to time to fulfill the promise of bringing about the international age. But the international age was not to belong exclusively to those espousing liberal-democratic ideals, instead it belongs to those who have the power and will to make it work in their own interests. For example if China is to be encouraged to participate in global markets then it is only natural that they will do so in a way that is more beneficial to them. Why should China agree to a game whose rules it had no say in shaping?

With great enthusiasm Canada has, at least on the surface, played a leading role in promoting international norms and rules. To the dismay of Canadians the latter half of 2018 made clear that the progress of Canada's work towards building the liberal dream has been nothing more than window dressing in a game of great power competition. While more examples could be found we will look at two that garnered the most media attention. The first incident was the Canada-Saudi Arabia diplomatic standoff and the second was the beginning of tensions between Canada and China over the Chinese company *Huawei* and its future in Canada.

The Canada-Saudi episode flared up so quickly that most media outlets struggled to make sense of what was actually going on. In short the dispute was supposedly over a statement made by Canada's foreign minister Chrystia Freeland. The statement was an expression of concerns that Canada had over Saudi Arabia arresting a number of prominent human rights activists. The activists had been vocal critics of Saudi government policy towards minorities and of the lack of progress made on reforms it had promised earlier. In a shocking display of political immaturity the Saudi government released a flurry of statements condemning Canada for daring to "meddle" in internal Saudi matters. The condemnations were followed by the expulsion of Canadian diplomats, withdrawing of financial investments, and canceling of student exchange programs. On top of this there were a number of "unofficial" statements made by members of the Saudi government who were not *officially* speaking on behalf of the government at the time; such statements were along the lines of statements that Canada risks welcoming "reprisals for its insolence," and accusations of human rights abuses by Canadians towards women and Indigenous peoples[44]. Although the whole episode seemed bizarre and for the most part the Saudi reaction was seen as ridiculously childish what was an extremely disheartening development was that Canada stood completely alone in its statements criticising Saudi Arabia. No Western ally of Canada came forward to back up Canada's initial statement defending human rights or even to condemn the Saudis for their overreaction. Canada's reputation as a defender of human rights had been proudly held up only to be greeted with the violent threats from a so called "friendly" nation and the sound of crickets from its closest allies.

After receiving such an unfriendly and undignified reaction from the Saudi regime one could be excused for assuming that Canada would rethink its association with Saudi Arabia but this did not happen. At the height of the diplomatic dispute the Canadian government fell under scrutiny by media and opposition parties over trade deals that it has continued to honor with the Saudi government. A number of Canadian weapons companies had been contracted to supply the Saudi Armed Forces with Canadian weapons and vehicles, the cost of which is

---

[44] One has to wonder how the Saudis received the news that the *National Inquiry into missing and murdered indigenous women and girls* accused the Canadian government of perpetrating "genocide" against indigenous people.

estimated to be worth billions of dollars in sales. When questioned whether or not in light of the diplomatic dispute the deal would be canceled Prime Minister Trudeau shied away from speaking too much on the matter. To the surprise of many the Canadian government rejected the possibility of canceling the deal because of claims that the previous government of Canada, under Prime Minister Harper, had signed a contract that was too costly to Canadians to break. Canada seemingly bowed to Saudi influence by not refusing to honor the deal which could have allowed Canada to once again assert itself as a defender of human rights.

To some the dispute with Saudi Arabia was a chance for Canada to not only stand up for its national dignity but for the ideals it holds so dear; the Saudi regime is notorious as being a violator of human rights including oppressing religious minorities and threatening and killing members of the media who are critical of its actions at home and abroad. On top of this the Saudi regime is accused by many as financing and supporting a number jihadist groups including Al-Qaeda and the Islamic State. This list of alleged crimes against humanity would be enough to make any other regime an absolute pariah on the world stage but there is one more mark of the record of the Saudi regime, its war in Yemen. For years the Saudi regime has been supporting armed forces fighting in the bloody Yemeni civil war. This seemingly forgotten war has been raging on since 2015 when the Saudi-backed regime was overthrown by the Houthis who are a religious sect opposed to Saudi rule in Yemen. After five years of fighting tens of thousands have been left dead and thousands more are wounded. To make matters worse Yemen faces widespread famine and millions risk starving to death. Saudi Arabia's involvement in the war has included financial and material support to forces is sees as reliable allies but has also included the use of overwhelming air power, backed by American surveillance and attack drones, and the deployment of Saudi troops in Yemen. Despite calls from the UN for a halt to the fighting and the beginning of a diplomatic process to settle the war the Saudi regime, and Houthi forces backed by Iran for that matter, has continued fighting. It would be naïve to expect a war to end so easily and it would be equally naïve to expect Saudi Arabia not to take actions it saw as necessary to its national interests. Unfortunately such wishful thinking is embodied in Canada's faith in the liberal world order. In reality Saudi Arabia is an ally of Western powers and plays a key role in combating Iranian influence in the Middle-East.

Unfortunately for Canada 2018 would not end until a second diplomatic standoff began and made clear that for all the good will it has shown to others over the years it has not purchased much beyond lofty ideals and the occasional international summit. The second episode is part of a much bigger trend and has much deeper existential consequences. The growth of Chinese financial and political power has resulted in America reassessing the uses and roles played by Chinese companies in areas of economic activity especially the realm of telecommunication. Chinese telecommunication companies have developed advanced technology that is extremely attractive to politicians, business people, and consumers alike. The rapidly advancing communication technologies that are hitting markets around the world are accompanied by equally advanced telecommunication infrastructure. The so called "internet of things" promises a world where consumer comfort and satisfaction is mastered by an increase in the personal data and information collected by devices. But in order to benefit from the full potential of the "internet of everything" there must be the necessary infrastructure to make the network possible. This is where *Huawei* comes in. As one of the world's leaders in "5G" technologies the company provides the public and governments alike with the future of telecommunication technology at an attractive price. The only problem with *Huawei*, as with most companies in China, is that there is an unsettling amount of influence by the Chinese Communist Party the company in terms of granting government access to technologies and information databases.

Actions taken on behalf of Canada's closest ally, the United States, has led to a standoff between Canada and China. Canada and China's dispute over Canada's decision to arrest the CEO of *Huawei*, one of China's largest "private" businesses and one of the largest telecommunications providers in the world, on behalf of the United States has forced Canadians to come to terms with the reality that there is a new global struggle being waged between America and China and that Canada is stuck right in the middle of it all. The struggle is one as old as recorded history; it has been fought again and again by the forces representing the status quo power and the rising power[45]. This episode signals the beginning of a more public competition between America and China over who will have control of world trade in the decades to come.

At the request of the American administration Canadian authorities arrested the CEO of the Chinese telecommunication company *Huawei* over claims of violations of American sanctions on Iran. The American sanctions have made it illegal under American law for companies doing business in America to carry on business relations directly or indirectly with Iran. Although the arrested CEO and the company have denied the allegations American prosecutors have started court proceedings including filing an extradition request with Canada to have the CEO, Meng Wanzhou, deported to the United States to stand trial. Canada and America have a long history of collaborating in matters of law enforcement including honoring extradition requests made by each other. The underlying question that seems to be driving events stems from security concerns surrounding *Huawei* and its involvement with building

---

[45] "More people worship the rising sun than the setting sun."
Sulla

telecommunication infrastructure in Canada. The alleged close ties the company has with the Chinese government leads some to believe that anything the company is involved with has the potential of becoming a tool of the Chinese government; Chinese government access to databases and lines of communication would present to it a vital asset in its struggle for more international influence. With American and Canadian relations becoming more continental it is not surprising that concerns over potential Chinese government infiltration into important infrastructure have caused American concerns and led to actions being taken to block such infiltration.

It is not unreasonable that, given the nature of modern communication technology, America would be concerned with the potential for an unfriendly government to intercept sensitive information. Advanced industrial societies thrive on more than just the movement of goods and people, the movement and collection of information has become the hallmark of the technological age. The rise of "big data" has become the life blood of modern economies. But in order to ensure that such handling of information is done for the benefit of its own society a country has to secure that the movement of information is not accessed and used by forces that would use the information to undermine said society. The development of advanced telecommunication technology, as with all past technology, will not be used exclusively for consumer purposes but will be utilized by governments and security forces. If America for example was to begin using new technology that would allow for its military forces to enjoy a higher degree of force projection then it would first be necessary to ensure that the technology being proposed does not leave forces vulnerable to disruption and interception by hostile forces. If the accusations against *Huawei* are true, that it works closely with Chinese authorities in the realms of law enforcement and intelligence gathering, then America, or any rival of China, would be foolish to use such technology that would leave them exposed to prying eyes. This rationale is argued by America in order to convince its allies not to use potentially compromised technologies in the building of new telecommunication infrastructure. Canada has been warned that its use of *Huawei* technologies in telecommunication infrastructure may leave Canada vulnerable to espionage and hostile cyber activities. By honoring America's extradition request Canada has seemingly agreed to protect American interests in preserving continental security in the realm of communication technologies.

The examples provided above serve as instances where liberal ideals have come up against the realities of international relations. Both episodes highlight a number of aspects of liberalism that are difficult to reconcile with realism: Canada is obligated to honor the free market by separating financial matters from political morality which is akin to selling out concerns of human rights; the Chinese company *Huawei* has the right to operate its business in compliance with Canadian business laws but this poses a risk to national and continental security matters; American law is not international law but Canada does recognize the legitimacy of the US legal system and the charges it lays. It is unclear how liberalism is going to be able to cope with international realism without deviating from core tenants of its thought; this is a problem for both the progressive and conservative schools of thought.

The world order born out of the ashes of the Second World War was brought into this world by American hands and since then has been nurtured by American sustenance. The order is more than just political policies tending towards liberal-democracy but it is much more importantly an ordering of society around a global free market based on certain accepted rules and norms. America has found it necessary to defend and expand global trade by means of opening free markets and organizing them in ways it sees fit. The defense of these markets and global trade in general is the very reason that America continues to be a super power. The economic benefits brought about through the defense of global trade have translated into a world that is more stable and has seen an overall uplifting of living conditions the world over. The cynic, or even Marxist, will say that America is only defending global trade in order to enrich itself, and while it is true that America itself is made richer by its defense of global trade it cannot be said that it is the only one benefiting from economic activity. We have to remember that ideologically America is a liberal state and the universalist nature of liberalism dictates that it must spread itself across the whole world. So yes, America does defend global markets for the wealth it produces but it also *needs* to defend global markets because it is in its nature to do so.

Some may ask why America should even bother continue being the *sole* arbiter of global trade when the system seems to be so well organized that it could probably do without American activity; wouldn't it be better to hand the order over to the international community so that all nations can have a greater say. Such a question misses the nature of global relations. If America was to retreat from its role as defender of global trade and norms then very quickly there would be a number of powers who would rush in to take up America's former positions. We in the West who are not a part of the political machinations of the system or in its defense tend to ignore that what we consider "our way of life" does come about all by its own. Our contemporary Western society is the product of forces that are enabled to exist because of immense political, economic, and military forces making it so. Pericles' warning to the Athenians, that "it is certainly dangerous to let it go," should be taken very seriously by those who enjoy what the liberal world order has to offer them.

While it is still early in the *Huawei* saga to determine what exactly will be the outcome it is clear that Canada is going to be closely watched by its American ally to determine if Canada is going to put continental security before vague notions of national sovereignty. If what we have been discussing has any validity then it is certain that from here on out Canada is going to be extremely cognizant of ulterior motives that Chinese business investments in this country may hold. We need only consider the history of security alliances to realize that all alliances hold within them the keys to their own destruction. The security arrangements protecting North America's continental integrity are only as strong as its weakest component. If China truly does intend to upend America's dominance of global trade then it will likely do so by fomenting unrest on the continent or seek to weaken America's political and economic ties with Canada and Mexico. The closer the continent moves towards political and economic integration the more secure America will be which will allow it to focus on its interests overseas.

Perhaps there are those Canadians who, out of their hatred of the current administration, would support policies which would damage President Trump's policies and by extension his presidency. But of course this will not happen. The relationship between the two countries is much too deep and Canada relies a great deal on America's wellbeing in order to allow Canada to function as a stable country. As elections in Canada go there does not seem to be any realistic chance of an anti-establishment or anti-American movement gaining any traction for this would mean a complete revolutionizing of

Canadian society from a liberal-democratic state with a free market economy to something which most Canadians would likely come to regret; Canada would lose the very thing that has allowed it to maintain at least formal independence, American goodwill based on Canadian partnership. If Canada was to suddenly pose a security threat to America then it would not be unreasonable to see America take the steps it deemed necessary in order to secure North American security; this could mean a breaking apart of Canadian confederation or instigating a political crisis requiring military intervention or it could simply be making moves to weaken the Canadian economy forcing Canada to come begging to forgiveness. But it is unlikely that these steps will ever be taken due to the nature of Canadian politics.

Much of what I have laid out above will likely seem farfetched to some readers especially when viewed from the point of view of liberal internationalism. If one takes an honest look at how international relations have developed since the end of the Cold War one finds that things have not played out the way that the optimists of the 1990's thought they would. There are obviously many positive developments that have come about since the 1990's: the advent of the internet has brought about an unprecedented level of international connectivity where the sharing of ideas is done instantly, medical breakthroughs have increased the average life spans of men and women around the world *and* at the same time the quality of living has improved into later life, increased trade has opened up new economic opportunities for millions of people. Clearly there has been progress made in the material condition of man. But it would be irresponsible to assume that everything has been "sunny ways." The march of time, despite popular opinion, is not inherently "moral" but tends to develop in directions dictated by existing powers. That nearly thirty years since the end of the Cold War in 1989 the world should find itself on the threshold of another Cold War where there is once again the possibility of a global thermonuclear war between nuclear armed states is testament to the constancy of human nature in space and time.

2020

Since writing this book in early 2019 there have been a number of earth shaking events that have reinforced the view I held of Canada at that time.

At the time of writing this present edition of my book the world remains in a state of uncertainty in the realms of international relations, global trade, and health care.

In the realm of international relations America and China are de facto waging a cold war. This conflict was not unforeseen nor was it inevitable. But as China has increasingly been enjoying more influence in the world and America has increasingly become more insecure in its omnipotence in international relations it was only a matter of time before some event would occur that would bring the rivalry between the two states to a head.

The global Covid-19 pandemic that has gripped the world since early spring of 2020 has resulted in a wave of political finger pointing over responsibility of the origin, spread, and handling of the health crisis. America is fully convinced that China is responsible for the outbreak of the Coronavirus and must be held accountable. China on the other hand has focused on the spreading of the virus and what measures were taken to combat the disease. China argues that while the virus may have originated on its soil, a "wetmarket" in the city of Wuhan being the "official" explanation given by authorities, its spread and the resulting pandemic has been caused by inadequate and negligent actions on the part of other countries. Whichever explanation one chooses to believe what is undeniable is that since the beginning of the global pandemic hundreds of thousands of people have dies and millions have been infected and that this is a moment where governments are going to be called to task for where they stand in terms of the rivalry between China and America.

As a result of the pandemic economies around the world have taken a near fatal hit due to the national lock-downs implemented to prevent the spread of Covid-19. Economic activity nearly came to a halt as stores and services were forced to close for an indefinite amount of time. Everything short of the purchasing of food and fuel was forced to stop. Most governments were able to take such steps as forcing the closure of businesses and restricting travel and social interaction by implementing unprecedented emergency powers to give them the authority to implement fines and make arrests to enforce the lock-down measures. In mid March 2020 a financial crisis began at the signal of historic drops in global stock markets and a few weeks later the world was greeted to near negative oil prices. If one was to take the time to look around and take it all in one would likely think the world was ending.

Where has Canada been placed because of the events of the global crisis? Canada remains firmly rooted where it was before the crisis. The 2019 general election resulted in a minority Liberal government but not much in the way of any policy changes. Much to the chagrin of China Prime Minister Trudeau seems just as committed as ever to upholding Canada's commitment to the liberal world order. Despite its moves of "goodwill" in the early stages of the global pandemic China does not seem to have made much headway in improving its reputation in Western countries. Canada, like many other countries, received large amounts of medical equipment from China is an apparent show of goodwill, however most of the equipment was deemed below standard and was rejected. What this episode showed was a dangerous vulnerability to not just Canada's health care industry but to all those countries who, because of globalization, have come to rely of China to supply them with life sustaining supplies.

Canada has been forced once again to look to its ally to the South in the realization that nations inevitably look out for their own interests. The political damage control campaign that China has been waging since the beginning of the pandemic has made clear that the liberal institutions built in the years following the Second World War pose a threat to liberal-democratic countries if they allow for the liberal ideology inherent in the institutions to be displaced my totalitarian and authoritarian regimes who have the economic muscle to do so.

The shape the world will take as the course of the global pandemic, geopolitical rivalry of America and China, and economic crisis continue to develop is uncertain. What is certain is that business as usual as was taken for granted in the post-Cold War and post-9/11 era has ended and a new reality is upon us. Because of circumstance continental integration will only accelerate as Canada is faced by an increasingly hostile China that is doubly angry over Canada's arrest of Meng Wanzhou and

America's attempts to place sole blame for the Coronavirus pandemic of the Chinese regime. If China's intention was to quietly gather strength and eventually displace American predominance by means of business deals and cultural exchange then America's attempts to draw a dividing line and make the contrasts between America and China more visible is an attempt to block the "peaceful" shifting of global power to East-Asia. If America's position in the world is threatened then everyone must understand that it won't go down without a fight; and Canada will play a major role in the outcome of that fight.

Conclusion

This book is not meant to be a lament for any nation. I consider it to be a bit childish and even potentially dangerous to hold the world view that finds one living in a state of ignorant bliss at the expense of understanding what is going towards making that very life style possible. Perhaps this is simply one of the internal contradictions of liberalism where individuality is worshiped but only because large and complex social, political, economic, and security arrangements make it possible. If anything has been made clear since the end of the Cold War it is that history marches based not on ideologies and ideals but on raw power and force.

Why lament for the disappearance of something which was destined to be crushed under the march of progress? The 19th century Europe which gave birth to Canada and its ideals was sacrificed upon the altar of the 20th century and burned up in the flames of war. The very ground out of which Canada sprung up out of has been forever devastated and salted leaving Canada thoroughly uprooted and unable to return to where it once was.

Canada is an archaic society but not because of what those on the far left and those who subscribe to "intersectionalism" would attribute to it. Canada is archaic because it is a country that was founded upon the best ideological intentions of 19th century liberalism and has since its founding been sheltered from the harsh realities of historical development in the old world. While 19ᵗʰ century developments in Europe saw the march towards the First World War developments in Canada and North America did not follow the same path. On the eve of the Great War North American society was ambitiously declaring the 20ᵗʰ century to be the "American/Canadian century" respectively by Americans and Canadians alike.

If the message of this book has come across as too harsh the reader should understand that it is not out of malice or disdain for Canada that I have said such things. All that was intended from this short book was to express some views on where Canada has ended up since George Grant's *Lament for a Nation*. What should be obvious to the reader is that in the pages of his book Grant correctly predicted the course of Canadian-American relations would take: that they would weather the comings and goings of alternatively popular and unpopular US administrations, that Canada would deepen its commitments to continental security, and that constant "progressive" developments changing Canadian society would once and for all alter it beyond its ability to retain a coherent national identity.

Canada is at once a sovereign liberal-democratic nation state and an integral part of North America's security apparatus. Canada enjoys the best of both worlds: American culture and economic prosperity without having to directly contribute too much to the empire beyond its commitments to collective security: Canada retains some aspects of its "European" political culture in the sense that it has a strong social welfare program: its social welfare programs receive additional funding because of the large security umbrella of America that allows the Canadian government to focus resources on domestic social issues: in return for the security umbrella Canada has certain obligations towards continental security including its roles in NATO and NORAD which work in Canada's interests anyway.

What remains uncertain is how Canada can expect to go on as an independent and sovereign country now that it has become so deeply entrenched in the American liberal order. In the decades to come Canada will face one of two possible fates each as damaging to its existence as the next: either the American liberal order will collapse and so with it Canada's *raison d'être* as a member of the "community of nations" as defined by the post-Second World War order, or alternatively, if the American order does not collapse but instead continues developing along its current historical trajectory then Canada as an independent nation state will become increasingly anachronistic in a world that is forever "progressing" towards universalism and globalism. Canada has become as much an ideological cause as it was a nation. If there is any nation existing on borrowed time it is Canada and this truly is lamentable.

Bibliography:

-Bickerton, J., Brooks, S., Gagnon, A. (2006) *Freedom Equality, Community: The Political Philosophy of Six Influential Canadians*. Quebec City: Mcgill-Queen's University Press

-Burke, E. (1987). *Reflections on the Revolution in France*. Indianapolis, Indiana: Hackett Publishing Inc.

-Clausewitz, C. (1982). *On War*. London: Penguin Books

-Creighton, D. (1971). *The Story of Canada*. Canada: Macmillan Company of Canada

-Grant, G. (1970). *Lament for a Nation*. Toronto: McClelland and Stewart Limited in association with the Institute of Canadian Studies, Carleton University

- Grant, G. (1969). *Technology and Empire*. Toronto: House of Anansi Press Limited

-Huntington, S. (2002). *The Clash of Civilizations*. London: Free Press

-Ignatieff, M. (2000) *The Rights Revolution*. Toronto: House of Anansi Press Limited

- Kennan, G. (1951). *American Diplomacy 1900-1950*. Chicago, Illinois: University of Chicago Press

-Machiavelli, N. (1992). *The Prince*. New York: Dover Publications

-Mearsheimer, J. (2003). *The Tragedy of Great Power Politics*. New York : W. W. Norton & Company

-Thucydides, (1972). *History of the Peloponnesian War*. London: Penguin Books

-Tocqueville, A. (1998). *Democracy in America*. Ware, Hertfordshire: Wordsworth Editions Limited Cumberland House

-Trudeau, P. (1968) *Federalism and the French Canadians*. Toronto: Macmillan Company of Canada

-Trudeau, P. (2010) *Approaches to Politics*. Toronto: Oxford University Press